Loss Adjustment

Published by Awa Press
Level Three, 67 Dixon Street, Wellington 6011, New Zealand

First published in Singapore by Ethos Books, 2019
Published with revisions by Awa Press, 2020

Copyright © Linda Collins 2019

ISBN 978-1-927249-70-3 (paperback)
ISBN 978-1-927249-71-0 (epub)
ISBN 978-1-927249-72-7 (mobi)

The right of Linda Collins to be identified as the author of this work in terms of Section 96 of the Copyright Act 1994 is hereby asserted.

This book is sold subject to the condition that it shall not, by way of trade or otherwise, be lent, resold, hired out or otherwise circulated without the publisher's prior consent in any form of binding or cover other than that in which it is published and without a similar condition including this condition being imposed on the subsequent purchaser.

A catalogue record for this book is available from the National Library of New Zealand.

Quote from "The Kingfishers" by Charles Olson
courtesy of University of California Press.
Quote from "Snow White and the Seven Dwarfs"
by Anne Sexton courtesy of Sterling Lord Literistic, Inc.
© 1981 Linda Gray Sexton and Loring Conant, Jr

Author photograph and photograph of
Victoria McLeod both courtesy of Malcolm McLeod
Cover design by Keely O'Shannessy
Typesetting by Tina Delceg
Editing by Mary Varnham

This book is typeset in Goudy
Printed in China by Everbest Printing Investment Limited

Produced with the assistance of

Awa Press is an independent, wholly New Zealand-owned company.
Find more of our award-winning and notable books at awapress.com.

Loss Adjustment

LINDA COLLINS

AWA PRESS

For Victoria

A NOTE TO THE READER

This is a true story of suicide and grief. If you find yourself feeling troubled or disturbed, we urge you to put down the book and talk to someone about how you feel. It is the author's hope that sharing her story will open up many conversations about mental health, especially among parents and their teenage children, and encourage people who experience suicidal feelings to seek help. A list of caring agencies is at the back of this book.

I have had nothing bad happen to me except my own doing. I have let this cowardice envelop me, and I can't shake it off. I will commit the worst thing you can ever do to someone who loves you: killing yourself. The scary thing is, I'm okay with that.

Victoria McLeod,
journal entry, March 30, 2014

LOSS

I

1

TIME TO WAKE UP

I get up at 6.45 a.m. to prepare breakfast for my seventeen-year-old daughter, Victoria. All over this tropical yet urbanised island of Singapore, mothers are rising to get their children ready for school. For our family, it is the first day of the second term of Victoria's final year at her school, an international one for expatriates. It is the day that exam results will be known.

The time, 6.45 a.m., is when I always get up during term time in order to get Victoria, our only child, breakfasted, dressed in her school uniform, teeth brushed, and then off downstairs to the 7.32 school bus. The evening before, she had laid out her school clothes on the dressing table in her bedroom to save time in the morning. I'd panicked that evening as I couldn't find socks with the school logo. Vic was amused by my panic and dug up two manky dust-covered socks from under her bed, saying, "Mu-um. These'll do." My husband Malcolm hauled out shoe polish from the cupboard under the sink and buffed Vic's brown lace-up school shoes with a ton of spit and energy. It was how his late dad, Jack McLeod, taught him to do it. It seemed important for Malcolm to pass this bit of Jack on to his daughter.

Malcolm had explained to Vic, "One day we won't be around to do all this stuff, like polishing shoes. Here's what you need to do." She smirked and did the eye-roll. "Da-ad."

Later, doing the dishes the old-fashioned way—by hand—they had a tea-towel fight. Vic could flick a mean tea-towel. She giggled as she caught Mal a good one on his arm. But she'd been unusually pensive during the day. She'd urged me to look at old photos of myself when I was young. I asked her, "Why would I want to look at those? I wasn't so happy then." And she said something about me being thin and pretty back then, which I took totally the wrong way, as if she was saying I was fat and ugly now. And later I wondered, if only I had asked her why she'd said that to me.

That morning I had woken up euphoric in the aftermath of a long dream in which Victoria was spinning in the universe and saying, "I'm free, free! I'm free. And you're free!" The dream seemed to have gone on for a long time. Vic was above the ground, her hair long and golden, her clothes light-coloured, the sky around her the bright blue of a kingfisher's wing. I was rising after her. She stretched out her hand to me. I was reaching for it, but already she was soaring away from me, looking upward, smiling. She was so happy. That was what had made me, in turn, euphoric. I was so happy she felt that way. I had woken up lying in the position Victoria always slept in—on her back, with her arms crossed behind her head, facing the room. Usually I sleep on my side. I am semi-comatose and grumpy when I awake. To have woken in this position, with my daughter's voice in my head telling me she is free, was disconcerting.

Instead of getting up, I had lain in bed and recalled the restless night I'd spent. At one point I'd woken to the TV still murmuring in the living room although it must have been about two a.m. Malcolm, a night owl, was up watching tennis. I got up and burst into the living room. Malcolm and our cat Mittens, on the sofa beside him, both looked up indignantly. I said it was school tomorrow, and it was already today, and in a couple of hours I had to get up and get ready. Malcolm shrugged good-naturedly and turned off the TV. I tiptoed into Vic's room and she seemed to be sleeping, although unusually she had pulled the covers over her head. I listened to her steady breathing and said the mantra for good luck that I always whispered to her last thing: "Good night, darling. Love you." Then I backed out quietly, shut the door, which gave an irritating clunk on the last turn of the knob, and went to sleep.

At 6.45 I recall all this and crack on with the morning. I get up, put the toast in the toaster, get the coffee ready and think, That's odd, Vic hasn't got up yet. It's nearly seven o'clock.

I go into her bedroom, calling, "Time to wake up, Vic." The curtains are still drawn, but sunlight through the gaps lets me see that the covers are folded back. Vic isn't there. I knock on the bathroom door. No reply. I open it. She isn't there. Maybe she is playing a silly trick and hiding in the cupboard under the sink. I look, full of hope, but she isn't there.

Maybe she is in one of the other rooms? I run to them. She isn't there. Maybe she is out on the balcony? She isn't there. I wake Malcolm, grab my phone and run downstairs. I start to run towards the hill leading to other apartment blocks. Something stops me. It is more than not wanting to go further from home. It is a feeling that I mustn't go there. I pull out my phone and text: "Please, Vic, where are you?" I run back to our apartment. As I run I allow myself, fearfully, to wonder if Vic has headed off to the main road for some reason, to go to where there is a bridge over a canal. Why would she do that? Why do I think she might do that?

In the apartment, Malcolm is pacing the rooms, bewildered. We hear the sound of a motorbike. We rush out, hoping for news. It is Mohan, the condominium's security guard. The burly man with a carefully tended moustache and a devotion to his job has known Vic since she was a little girl. This familiar kindly man, in his blue uniform and polished black shoes, is sobbing.

Mohan won't tell us what is wrong. He is shaking, burying his head in his hands, saying only, "Come.

You must come. Over the hill, over the hill." He has come to get us, to take us there. We don't want to go. We cling to what should be. The school bus will be here soon. We want it to be there. I want to call out, "Victoria, the bus is here," to see her emerge from her bedroom, hauling her green school backpack over her shoulders, bending like an old woman lugging all her belongings on her back, then straightening to stand tall and beautiful; to see her in the shiny polished shoes, the laces done up haphazardly; to pat her on the back as she goes out the door, an habitual gesture for luck with a prayer to keep her safe, that I always do; and to see Mittens dash out and after her down the stairs as she always does.

Tabby-coloured Mittens and black-coated Angelina have run out on to the balcony, confused and scared. Dread rakes my stomach like cats' claws. "You must come," Mohan repeats. We are shepherded downstairs to the carpark. We are silent, made mute. We go forth helplessly, to what we fear at some visceral level is our death, or at least the death of our current selves. We will go wherever we are led for we are powerless.

We find ourselves in a white SUV that Mohan has flagged down. He instructs the driver to go to the apartment block on the other side of the hill. The driver nods, realising it is an emergency. We travel along the road, past families in their homes getting ready for the day. We arrive at the other side of the hill and pull up near an apartment block facing tropical angsana and tembusu trees and pink and white bougainvillea. A crowd has gathered at the foot of this apartment building. They are Singaporeans of all ages and some young Filipina domestic helpers who are holding each other and crying. Police sit on motorbikes, or else stand about, making notes or speaking into phones. Yellow crime-scene tape keeps the crowd back from the object of their attention.

She lies on her back, with her arms crossed behind her head, on the buff-coloured concrete tiles of a path leading from the ground-level carpark to the lobby. Her beautiful face is thin and drained. Her eyes are closed. Her neck is at an angle and an arm is oddly twisted. You do an everyday thing like get out of a car. You see a person, still and empty. You have the overwhelming sense of something precious gone from the world. What remains is a body that resembles your daughter. But it can't be.

Victoria is alive and tall, and the sun would glint on her hair now, if it were her. But the body of this person has— inexplicably—hair of the darkest brown. The place where she lies is still in shadow. There are sticky thick dark-red stains on the tiles. Perhaps, perhaps, she is asleep, in the shade but facing towards the things she loves—the sun, nature—as the kingfisher and white-crested thrushes shriek, as the morning heat already starts to rise from the ground. But I know she is not really asleep. My stomach flips and I rush towards the body. Police stop me. I must wait for the inspector to arrive, they say firmly. Malcolm, sobbing, choking, saying over and over again, "No, no, no, no, Victoria," manages to break free. He rushes up to Victoria and—thank God—he kisses her face as he weeps. A policeman drags him away.

We are both made to sit in chairs borrowed from a nearby apartment. We face our dead child about fifty metres away, as the heat and the ants come, as people stare and point. Malcolm is next to me, saying over and over in anguish, "No. No. No." Unable to bear this inhuman arrangement, he tries to stand and walk away, then turns back and grabs Mohan, who is still with us. He is in Mohan's great bear arms; they howl together. I sit numbly, disbelieving. I wonder why I don't cry. I wonder if this is me being the "sensible" one in the relationship. I would prefer it if I could stand up and scream and go mad and be taken away somewhere. But some part of me that is the dutiful daughter, the obedient person, the stoic, the loyal mother, keeps me in the seat, in this ludicrous position, staring at my dead daughter.

The police are erecting a little blue tent that they will use to cover the body. I hope that Victoria will stand up and say, "Fooled you! Time to go camping."

A white van turns up to take her to the morgue. I should be with her. They won't let us go. Malcolm and I find ourselves back at our apartment. The police are asking us questions. "Did you know she was at this block?" one asks, aggressively. We wonder why we are asked such a stupid question. What do they mean? They frown and prowl around the living room and Victoria's bedroom. They examine the books on her desk. When we follow them, they tell us to sit and wait on the sofa. Then the inspector takes a call. He smiles and says Vic's phone and slippers have been found on the tenth storey and it looks like there are no suspicious circumstances. I nod. They could say anything and I would nod. They seem relieved. I realise dimly that in their eyes we are no longer murderers.

They ask us to come with them into Victoria's room, to answer questions about its contents. Vic's school clothes are still laid out on her desk; her shiny brown shoes are next to her schoolbag. There are presents for a friend's birthday, all wrapped up. The police take those. We are over-eager to help, as if being nice to the police will make them go away—will make it all go away. No suicide note, though. There must be one somewhere, I hope. A last message to us. I do find a little yellow Post-it in Vic's handbag. In tiny neat handwriting it says: "I don't want to be left a vegetable." The police take it, along with her notebooks, her camera and her laptop. Then they depart, a great rush of heaviness leaving the house. It is empty, except for Malcolm and me on the sofa, shaking and weeping, occasionally looking up to stare at each other in disbelief.

2

GOOD MORNING

Hours pass. I surface, restless. Domestic chores provide a comfort. I become a worker ant. I sweep up around the cats' bowls. The floor still isn't clean enough. When I bend down and peer closely at the marble tiles, there is a line of tiny black ants oscillating between the two tin cat bowls and a small gap in the skirting. I take the bowls to the sink, where I viciously scrub off hardened nubs of Fancy Feast Grilled Ocean Whitefish and Tuna Feast in Gravy. I spray disinfectant on the floor where the bowls sit, sending the black line into a panic. On my hands and knees, I crush the ants with a white kitchen towel emblazoned with the words *Good Morning* and then throw it in the rubbish.

The feeling of the cloth in my hands is a reminder there is washing to be done. Peering into the washing machine, I see a brown T-shirt of Victoria's. One of her last acts has been to put it there. Why would anyone leave a T-shirt to be washed when they are going to kill themselves and have no need of it any more? I think this only fleetingly as I cry out with a mangled joy at the sight of this relic and press the soft cloth to my face. The T-shirt is strangely slick with sweat. I inhale the smell of Victoria, of youth and sour anxiety and sweet, sickly Taylor Swift perfume. Under what circumstances did she wear it in the hours after I said good night to her not even twelve hours ago? Had she slipped outside, gone to the ledge, endured agonising turmoil, then decided against the end, run back home and gone back to bed? Then woken later, to try again in different clothes and perhaps, in some warped act of kindness for me, done this simple domestic chore before quietly closing the front door and going into that dark night? Not an expression of a lingering desire to live, to see a future where clothing would be washed for another wearing, so much as a last gesture of love?

I want to run to wherever the police have taken her and hold her tight and tell her, "There, there, Mummy's here, no need to be afraid." And then I realise I may never again hold her and inhale her smell. This T-shirt is the last of her I will ever have. I put it in a plastic bag and place it in a dressing-table drawer of nightwear, tucking it at the very back. It will be my secret cache when the need to touch and smell something of Victoria becomes unbearable. I think all these things quickly and shut the drawer on that future for now. That future, which is life with a dead child. For now, she is not dead. She's here, somewhere. I have just mislaid her.

———

I'm not sure what to do after that. It feels as if someone has punched me in the head. I can't focus. It takes a long time to formulate a thought. What do people do in a crisis? On that old British soap opera *Coronation Street*, which I used to watch on black and white TV when I was little, sensible Ena Sharples would make a cup of tea. I make Malcolm a cup of tea, which he is incapable of drinking, or even acknowledging, as he sits on the sofa staring into space. Then I realise Ena Sharples would not have made a cup of tea—that tough old battle-axe from Manchester would have gone to the Rovers Return and downed a pint of stout.

I am not one for beer in a crisis, though. I like the ritual of making tea: the boiling of the kettle, the rustling up of a teabag, the stirring of sugar. I feel soothed. I allow myself to think about a little bit of the future—such as the next hour.

Monday is always a day off work for me. Normally by now, 11 a.m., I would have come back from a long walk and showered. I would be planning what I would cook for dinner, and what I'd have ready for Vic to eat when she arrived back home on the school bus at 4.20. She likes store-bought treats such as brownies and cinnamon buns, or homemade items such as banana bread, or melted cheese on toast. She is at school, right? It's easiest to pretend this is so, although Malcolm has now gone into her room and is crying and repeating, "Oh no, no, no." Normally at this time he would still be asleep as he works nights as deputy picture editor at *The Straits Times*. I would be quiet around the house so as not to wake him.

Even though he is quite awake and crying loudly, instead of going to comfort him I go to my laptop on the dining table in the living room. I decide not to check my emails. I might feel that I would have to write and send some, saying what has happened. How do I even begin to say that I have lost the person who made my life worth living? That my own flesh and blood decided life was so awful that they forced themselves to do this most unnatural thing, destroying themselves in an act of unimaginable fear and pain and loneliness? That it seems a total rejection of me as a mother and all the love I thought we shared? That the daughter I thought I knew was a complete stranger?

Instead, I go to the documents folder and call up architect plans and costing specifications, in what has become a daily ritual for over three years, since an earthquake in February 2011 destroyed our house in Christchurch. We were in Singapore when the earthquake struck, lucky enough to be spared that particular trauma. The house was rented out. The insurer has finally agreed to build a replacement house. I look at costings for door handles. I'm aware, dimly, that there is no future now, that I no longer have a family who could live in the imagined house. Victoria had marked one of the downstairs bedrooms as hers as it would have its own separate entrance, which would be great when she was studying at university. The new reality is a brutal truth for another time. Vic would prefer a clean-edged lever door handle in chrome, I decide, forcefully. The decision feels like a triumph. I can control this one small thing, while my life as I have known it topples.

3

AFTERNOON

It is about four hours since I saw Vic's broken body on the tiles at the bottom of the apartment block. The sun outside is burning even more brightly than when we were sitting on chairs as a crowd looked on and the ants streamed out towards her.

Malcolm emerges from the bedroom. We hug each other. Then he looks at me and says, "We have to tell people."

I send out the first email at 2.58. I think there were phone calls made before that. I can't remember. Is it family or close friends I message? No, for some reason I send the first email to someone I don't even know, the organiser of a tennis match I am due to play the following day: "Hi, I am afraid I can't play tomorrow. I have suffered a sudden bereavement. I am in no state to find a sub, can you kindly do this for me. This is all I can manage at this stage. Linda."

It starts off formally but starts to wobble near the end. I'm still desperately trying to maintain some control over my life. I suppose by messaging the tennis organiser first I'm compartmentalising Vic's death into something affecting other people in terms of time and their convenience. It is a profoundly deluded thing to do. Five minutes later, this dip into the unfathomable—the act of notifying people—enables me to email a close friend in Wales: "Hi Jenny, dear Victoria is dead. she committed suicide. jumped off an apartment block at our condo. police have just gone. please send me prayers. Linda." That is more like the reality. However, the police left hours earlier, unless they have come back. I just can't remember, except that later in the afternoon word has spread and phone calls and emails start to come in.

During that day, and the day after, kind Singapore colleagues appear unbidden, to help. Siong, a subeditor I've known for years, who has put up with my outbursts of temper and cultural gaffes as a bumbling foreigner, and her husband Yoga, a night editor before his retirement, take care of the transportation as we have no car. There is a constant ferrying to and from the funeral parlour in town, after the visit to the morgue to formally identify the body. There are the police to check with, funeral details to organise, family to be picked up at the airport. Siong and Yoga take care of all of this with the help of other colleagues. We are only dimly aware. We are incapable of functioning. Shock has taken us far away. We have to be led by the hand like children from Siong and Yoga's car to the morgue and its administration office, to the embalmer, to the funeral parlour. Someone takes us to the doctor, where we are prescribed pills to make us sleep and to keep us sedated so the awfulness does not overwhelm us and make us run to the edge and jump, too.

4

NEXT

I have never before met the New Zealand High Commission's consular adviser Susan Woods, but I let this stranger, this helper of needy Kiwis, hold my hand as we walk into the morgue at Singapore General Hospital. We encounter a shabby, lino-floored public service office. Straight away, sweaty desperate men come up, tugging our clothes, murmuring into our ears and thrusting business cards at us. "Touts," someone explains. The men are paid by funeral homes to hang around the morgue and plead for business. I stare at them in a daze. Malcolm holds my other hand. I lean on to his shoulder.

"Are you ready?" I hear, from Susan.

I nod.

We proceed into a glassed corridor. Through the glass on our left I see stiff raised arms. The hands are clenched rigidly, as if protesting in anger. I see blue-grey eyes, now open and fixed. I see freckles. Tiny pale-brown dots across porcelain. The glass between us gives the illusion of a screen. I am a watcher, observing events.

This isn't real. A creature lies on the gurney. It is an upturned bird, with its claws tightly bent, dead on the floor of a cage.

"Do you identify this person as Victoria Skye Pringle McLeod?"

"Yes," blurts straight away from somewhere within me.

Susan grips my hand.

5

DRESSED

We are barely capable of figuring out how to get through the next hour, let alone organise our daughter's funeral. Colleagues from the newspaper step into the breach and arrange the rituals to send Victoria on her way. They check: Do you want her body flown to New Zealand and the funeral service held there? We both shake our heads. We know this much: Vic was born in Singapore; she died here. A large piece of her heart belongs to Singapore, even if her passport says she is a New Zealand citizen. Vic should be honoured, mourned and farewelled here. A memorial service for her in New Zealand can be held later.

Singapore is fitting for Victoria, but I realise later that if we had buried her in Ōamaru, Malcolm's hometown where her beloved Grandma Sheila lives, at least there would have been a gathering after the funeral that would have been a comfort. Old friends from our holiday home community in Kakanui would have come with food and drink to support us, express condolences and reminisce about Victoria. They understand the impermanence of life. The brother of one of Malcolm's friends took his own life. And Laura, the partner of another old friend, still grieves for her young sister, who at fourteen shot herself with her father's farm gun at the thought of having to return to boarding school for a new term. I find myself missing these understanding people, the sharing of a bottle of single malt whisky, the declarations of blasphemy (*Why, God? You motherfucker*), the Kiwi irreverence.

We arrive at the funeral home, the Singapore Casket Company. It is located in downtown Lavender Street and one of the most well-known and highly regarded of the many available. From the outside it could be a small hotel, like the ones nearby in the downtown area of the city that cater to tourists looking for affordable rooms. Smart enough, but not swanky. Malcolm is guided into what appears to be a lift lobby, but I am steered around to the other end of the building. I encounter an industrial scene of station wagons and vans backed up to a platform where bodies are removed and put on tables or gurneys, I can't remember which. Figures go about their jobs amid the engine roar of vehicles and clanging of steel on concrete. The factory element of the scene reminds me of the pre-digital heyday of newspapers, where deafening, shuddering presses turned out still warm editions that were loaded into delivery trucks.

Someone takes me to an area where a woman is moving about my daughter's body in some sort of professional role, judging by her precise practised movements. An embalmer, I suppose. The body is covered with a sheet, but there is Victoria's face, eyes finally closed, looking serene. I caress her forehead. It is marble cold. She has never been this cold. To think it was always fever I dreaded.

The woman moves with an intimate familiarity, lifting the sheet to show the body. My daughter is wearing only a bra and pants. This unexpected sight and the informality shock me. At the same time, I am grateful it is a woman tending to Victoria and not a male. She is indeed the embalmer, and she gives me a warm and encouraging smile that enables me to proceed rather than collapse screaming and sobbing, which I am afraid I may do. We are women in this together, an ancient task of womankind: dressing a dead child for a funeral. I steel myself to honour Victoria by performing with reverence this act of love, one of the last acts of physical touch I will ever experience with my daughter.

What did I dress my daughter in? I remember packing clothes, hair things and make-up off her dressing table. I can't remember much of how I washed her fine, long hair and then brushed it straight until it dried, but it would have been carried out tenderly, longingly, lingeringly. With plenty of kisses on those lifeless cheeks.

Afterwards, I am in the lobby of the funeral home. As I enter, led by Siong and Yoga, I notice there are several wakes taking place. In the Singaporean Chinese tradition, rooms and corridors are lined with large formal floral tributes mounted on plinths. These have been purchased by well-wishers, and have labels naming the deceased and the purchaser of the tribute. Victoria lies in the funeral home's Sapphire Room (complete with audiovisual facilities and tea- and coffee-making machines) and we, too, have floral tributes lining our corridor and room. They are from colleagues from newswire agencies and Singapore Press Holdings, including one from our editor, Warren Fernandez, a reminder of the workplace outside our little world of family grief. It is a reminder that this world of grief is different. In the West, death is often hidden away and the ritual of mourning done almost furtively and quickly so those left behind can "move on". There I would have found these brazen declarations of condolence tasteless, ersatz. However, here in Singapore, unmoored from my own culture and desperate for guidance, I feel buoyed by the sight of fragile petals and stems, and by the tributes that spell out our daughter's name. The names on the bouquets—Victoria's, our own and those of the condolence-givers—prove that she did and does exist. That we are still a family. That I have a wider family, of work colleagues. They anchor me.

We enter the Sapphire Room. It is small, tiled, windowless. On one wall is a large banner quoting St John about the way, the truth and the resurrection. Someone well-meaning has told the funeral home we are Christian. The casket company would have needed to know. I haven't thought of myself as Christian for many decades, not since my Catholic schooldays. My life has telescoped to merely earthly concerns.

Then I see Victoria. She is lying in a white coffin, stretched out with closed eyes. I cry out her name and rush to hold her, the pleasure at being with her again in any earthly form outweighing the fact she lies there dead.

6

THREE DAYS

In the West a wake usually follows a funeral. People gather for dainty sandwiches and cups of tea, and perhaps a tot of whisky. Condolences are offered to the bereaved. People hug, exchange brief memories, shed tears. And then they get into their cars and drive off. But we are in Singapore and a Chinese-style wake—with Christian elements—has been decreed for the duration of three days before the funeral. Malcolm and I are so bereft with grief that work colleagues, most of whom are Chinese, have kindly stepped in to help organise things.

Victoria is in an open coffin, as is the local custom, with photographs and memorabilia at the front of it. Mourners will keep her body company night and day until the funeral service and cremation. Malcolm's friend, a veteran photographer called Francis Ong, begins discreetly orchestrating the running of the room in which Vic lies. He has put his faith in a young photographer, Mark Cheong, placing him at the entrance for a demanding role requiring tact and a light but firm touch. The job is to man the visitors' book and ask for financial contributions for the bereaved. Every detail and amount will be meticulously recorded, and the process carried out with respectful good humour. We had no idea this would happen. To Westerners, the wrangling of money from visitors to the funeral home may seem a step too far. But later we are grateful for this pragmatism: the wake and funeral service cost over fifteen thousand dollars.

Mourners—and Singaporeans are all old hands at this grief business—have already started arriving. They sit in café-style chairs at circular tables. It could be a shophouse eatery, except the room is festooned with flowers and there is the matter of the coffin and its body. This does not deter the mourners from eating. Over the next three days they will eat and drink and crack melon seeds between their teeth and cry with us and laugh with us at memories of sad and happy times. They see it as perfectly normal for me to sit beside Victoria's body for hours on end, telling her how much I love her and all the things I meant to inform her of but never got around to. How her grandfather Jack was a conscientious objector in the Second World War but did not want to be separated from his mates and so became an ambulance officer. How Grandma Sheila recalls him waking from a frequent dream of the war, crying out, "I can't reach him, I can't reach him." I tell her he was a brave man who did the best he could within his own principles, how he would have loved her and been so proud of her. I ask her to tell Jack we miss him.

Days pass. I sit, hair dishevelled, face bare of make-up but streaked with tears. I don't care what I have got on, what shoes I'm wearing. Once or twice, when I am lifted gently by the arms to come and meet well-wishers, I see a look of shock at my appearance flash across their faces. One media colleague even sends a message that is relayed to me: "Tell Linda to at least do her hair for the funeral." The more traditional Taoists among the Chinese might approve my dishevelment: their rituals include having the immediate family wear sackcloth. Then again, elders are not expected to show respect to younger ones—in ancient times a child would have been buried in silence, without the palaver we are going through.

So that is who I am now, I think: a woman made mad, frumpy and unfashionably middle-aged by trauma and grief. However, I am mostly glad they can see my suffering, for I need to know through their eyes that I am suffering. I can't see it myself. I am too numb for that sort of awareness.

Who comes to say goodbye to my daughter, who has the courage or love or sense of decorum to participate in this rite of passage? Mostly it is colleagues, Singaporeans, who rise to the occasion. They know Malcolm and me through work and the occasional social gathering, yet their comfort at the wake is that of intimate fellowship.

Their understanding of grief is profound and respectful. Reporter Serene Goh, mother of a young child, stands near the coffin as a hush falls on the room, and sings from her heart a hymn for the grieving, "It Is Well With My Soul". Pat Daniel, then editor-in-chief of the English, Malay and Tamil media arm of my employer, Singapore Press Holdings, fills the little room with the bulk of his presence, then fills it again with a rendition of "Amazing Grace". His gravelly tenor is surprising in its sweet strength. It unites us, giving voice to the emotion we want to express, helping us to release our tears.

Mourners of all religions come. Muslim colleagues—whose own rites would not include a viewing time before the funeral as Islamic law decrees a body should be buried as soon as possible after death—come to this room with its Christian cross on a wall. One of them, Malcolm's friend Ishak, tells him to be strong. Be strong—it is also a saying of New Zealand Māori: Kia kaha. My husband repeats to himself: *Be strong*, as if trying it on for size. Yet he is finding it impossible to be strong. He realises that Ishak's advice is that of a believer, one who sees a point to all this suffering. A superior being has willed it and there is life after death. Malcolm admires that certainty, that belief. But he does not share it.

Singaporean neighbours come, and others who know me slightly through a newspaper column I used to write, and who have read of our daughter's death in a large *In Memoriam* notice we have placed in *The Straits Times*. Finally, some Westerners come: neighbours I haven't spoken to for years, mothers whose children played with Victoria when she was younger. I can tell they are shocked by the set-up—the swirl of Asian mourners, the donations entered into a ledger book at the entrance, the small room crowded with round tables and chairs, the open coffin, the dominance of Victoria's broken body as a focal point, the photos of her on prominent display. Shocked, too, at the sight of us alternately kissing Vic then shaking visitors' hands, and the faint cloying smell of dying flowers from another room, and joss sticks lit by who knows. But these women put aside any Western misgivings to embrace me, cry with me, and even talk quietly to Victoria in her coffin.

No one from Victoria's school visits, as far as we are aware: no teacher, principal, or even any of her friends. We are bewildered. We keep hoping someone will appear.

Days pass. We go back and forth between the funeral home and our apartment at various points of each day, returning home to draw breath. This lingering goodbye is perfect. The only way I'm able to keep going is to know I'll soon be back with Victoria, sitting with her in the funeral home, still having her physically in my life.

One day, the student welfare officer at Vic's school and her boss come to our home. I vaguely recall the boss from Vic's primary school years but don't know the other person at all. Why do these people, in particular, come from the school, a private one catering to international students? Why not a teacher Victoria especially liked, or the principal, or the deputy principal who led the choir our daughter sang in? But we do the decent thing, invite them in, and someone gets them a cup of tea. The student welfare officer is exceedingly well-dressed and coiffured, and clearly nervous. She and the other woman keep glancing at each other with apprehension as they ask how we are and tell us how shocked they are. There are awkward pauses. It seems as if they are expecting me to be angry with them or be asking them something. I put away the doubts that keep surfacing. For now, all I can deal with is kindness. Afterwards Malcolm and I say to each other, "That was unpleasant. Who were they? Perhaps they really liked Victoria? But why were they so anxious, rather than sad?"

Neighbours come to our home, Christian, Muslim, Buddhist and Taoist, each with their own kindness. A pastor comes and says prayers. Even Malcolm, a confirmed unbeliever, joins in. But he draws the line at one group of strangers who knock, offering to come in and comfort us, and sends them away. We later find out they were not a bunch of well-meaning, happy-clappy "God-botherers" as Malcolm had thought, but a group from the Samaritans of Singapore, who specialise in assisting those affected by suicide.

Flowers come: each knock at the front door reveals a scowling courier bearing a wreath or bouquet. The couriers are fed up at having got lost in the twists and turns of the large apartment complex.

Some people do not come. My parents in New Zealand are elderly and too frail to make the trip to Singapore. They send a huge bouquet of orchids in Victoria's favourite colour, purple. From my only sibling Peter and his wife and two sons there is silence. No phone call, not even an email. I phone and ask my mother, who lives close by them in Auckland, and she says they do not want to contact me. Apparently, their youngest boy (a year older than Victoria, with whom she played as a toddler whenever we made the long trek to New Zealand) says he hardly knew her and why bother. My mother does not seem to think this an outrage. Parents have their own reasons for what they say and who they are, and I had always loved them even if they seemed dismissive, but that day I realise a horrible truth: possibly they love me, but they really don't like me. It feels like I am losing not just my daughter, but my family.

If my family seem like outsiders, Malcolm's mother Sheila, in her late eighties, shares her heartfelt grief and wise words of comfort down the phone line from Ōamaru. Malcolm's sisters Sharyn and Paula fly to us from Sydney and Dunedin respectively. And Fiona Barrett, my best friend from high school at St Dominic's College, comes from Auckland. Kind friends pay her airfare. We see in the faces of Sharyn, Paula and Fiona our own bewilderment, shock and disbelief. We hug each other for strength.

Food comes. The women in my mostly British social tennis group draw up a roster and have someone drop off a home-cooked meal each night. This becomes a tiny welcome focal point for Malcolm and me: What have the tennis ladies delivered tonight? We marvel at a bagel brand we haven't seen before, and a colourfully layered vegetarian lasagne. Even if we are too sick with grief to eat, the practical gesture of support is welcome. And the food is not wasted. Asian neighbours and colleagues pop by to keep an eye on us, and bring food. It is good to emerge from our state of shock and offer them food and drink too, to partake in the ritual of being hosts, without the need for conversation that travels into the unfamiliar territory of deep loss, trauma and the nature of death itself.

Large foil roasting dishes containing penne pasta draped in velvet-textured sauces and roasted vegetables aromatic with balsamic vinegar (whipped up by a neighbour) sit next to a tureen of minestrone soup (senior editor Alan John) sit next to a tureen of pumpkin coconut soup (tennis ladies) and numerous hawker-centre plastic containers of seafood noodles, fried rice, steamed rice, roast pork rice, steamed wonton and braised kailan greens (journalists and photographers). A bag of three-in-one instant coffee mix has been placed on the kitchen benchtop. Drink cartons are everywhere: local brand Fraser & Neave's soy milk and chrysanthemum tea.

Our apartment has never been so full of food and people. *Straits Times* colleagues mill around, constantly checking their phones and eating food or going out to get it and bringing it back. Some attend to the door, letting people in and out. Some tend to the cats, putting food in their bowls and patting and stroking Mittens, the friendlier of the two. Siong and Yoga (whom Fiona mistakenly calls Yoda, like the *Star Wars* character) come with more food. Amid this constant physical presence of fellow human beings we gaze inward, trying to absorb what has happened with our lives and why the person we love the most is not here.

At some point Alan John sits down and coughs in a way that signals something important is going to be said. Alan is someone I don't really know except as my one-time boss, a Singaporean Indian who is a legend among Singapore journalists for his persistence in getting a story, his clear and compelling way of writing and his meticulous craftwork. He has a blazing don't-mess-with-me stare, yet I found him a person of compassion and understanding when I once sought his help because I had doubts about my worth as a copyeditor for the newspaper.

"Er-hem," he coughs. "Linda, Malcolm, forgive me, this needs to be asked. Have you thought about what service you want for Victoria?"

We wait for him to continue. We can't think of a funeral. The choice of songs. The cremation (burials are rare in land-scarce Singapore). All this is utterly unimaginable. He offers suggestions. We nod, not really hearing. Something about the school having people there, speeches.

The wake is a miracle amid the maelstrom. Victoria is dead but her body is still here, lying in a white coffin. This puts off losing her physical presence forever. I fear becoming a rip-off of a Henry Moore mother-child sculpture with a hole in the centre. The cremation is on Good Friday and then I won't have an object that is part of me yet separate from me any more. There'll just be a void.

If we had flown Victoria to New Zealand she would have been in a funeral home with private viewings in an atmosphere of stilted, muffled unquiet. I would have had little opportunity to sit with her and pour out my lamentations. The Singaporeans would not have been there with their reassuring ease in the ritual of mourning. My family might have come and rent the air with accusations and blame. Some mourners would have been embarrassed by my tears. They and others would have wanted the whole thing done and dusted quickly. The funeral director or an assistant might have been the ones dressing the body. I would not have realised the normality of death so quickly—and, more importantly, the necessity to go briefly mad with grief, to cover yourself, metaphorically, in the dowdy burlap of mourning.

7

GOOD FRIDAY

It's the third and final day of the wake—Chinese funerals are held for an odd number of days. Some say this is because even numbers are associated with joyful occasions. Others say it signifies life's incompleteness.

Today is also Good Friday, which is a much more formal occasion than in New Zealand. It is not just a public holiday where the point is to have fun and relax. Singapore society takes care to respect religious anniversaries and is scrupulous at allowing each religion its due in the interests of overall harmony. In my adrift state, the outsized quotation from the Gospel of John on the wall behind Victoria's coffin—"I am the resurrection and the life. Who believes in me will live even when he dies"—sears into my consciousness, at first in the form of an unwelcome guilt trip. It seems to have little connection with the reality before us. I realise with a start, though, that secretly I would love the stuff about the resurrection to be true. I would give anything to see Victoria again. Or at least to know there's a place where her soul is happy and safe. The icing on the cake would be angels, fluffy clouds and harps.

But in Singapore the afterlife is viewed through a different lens. The Chinese—well, non-Christian Chinese Singaporeans, and some Christians among them, too, I suspect—see death as a disruption to the cosmos, and the funeral rituals go some way towards restoring order and harmony. Harmony and order are seen as good for families, good for business, and good for creating the optimum conditions for humans to flourish. I'd like to think part of this "harmony" includes a continued, if different, relationship with the newly dead, yet it seems deluded in the twenty-first century to want to believe that Victoria is now up there, wherever *there* is, with ancestors who welcome her into a cosmos that may or may not contain the god of my Catholic upbringing.

Did Victoria even believe in God? We woefully neglected her spirituality, as indeed we neglected our own. For my part, it was not through any arrived-at rejection of God, or a Catholic god, or organised religion, or the Buddhist and Taoist beliefs around me. I was happy not to question why people would leave food offerings and burn fake money for their wandering loved ones during Hungry Ghost Month, which occurs in the seventh month on the lunar calendar (around August), when the gates of hell supposedly open to let the dead roam the Earth.

Belief in a Christian god was a matter I had no time to consider. I was too busy doing housework, checking

Vic had done her homework, preparing meals, dealing with builders and insurers (and lawyers and engineers and the Christchurch City Council), paying bills and doing editing. The day-to-day nature of living took precedence over any consideration of an afterlife.

Even now in the funeral home, as I look at my daughter's dead body and recall the terrible circumstances of her self-destruction, I don't feel a need to rail against a god who would do this. The most significant thing I believe right now is that today is the day of Victoria's funeral, that this is the last day I will see her physically, and that even the fleeting acknowledgement that this day will come to an end and that a new unwanted life is beginning is too much to bear. So I retreat. Let's see: I do know that today someone the Western world knows as Jesus Christ was crucified on a cross in Jerusalem. He rose again on the third day from the dead. However, I have no hope of that for my Victoria, even as I caress and kiss her corpse and murmur, "Why have you left me all alone? Please come back." Her soul has gone from it. I feel strongly that it does not want to return. I revisit the voice that spoke to me in a dream the morning Vic died. The only comfort is to believe it was her telling me, "I'm free, I'm free."

8

ROSE PETALS

Sharyn, Paula and I dress Victoria for her public display at the funeral, which is to take place several miles away at the crematorium later that day. We choose a bright melon-orange asymmetrical skirt from the ubiquitous Cotton On fashion chain, a skirt that she loved. She'd worn it when the family got together on Christmas Day 2012 at Paula and her husband Jim's holiday cottage in Central Otago. Jim took a photo of us with Victoria in centre spot, her vivid skirt a flag of youth and hope. That day, she wore a pair of buff-coloured ankle boots; she loved her boots and they gave her outfits an edge. With her blonde hair draping her shoulders and her dimpled cheeks peachy with health, she stares from the photo in what I now see is a mocking way. I am starting to suspect that the demons that drove her to despair were probably there already, unknown to us, behind the lovely smile for Uncle Jim's camera.

We put the photo among others on a small table at the end of the coffin; the Singaporean visitors like to look at the photos and comment, completely at ease in talking about my dead daughter as she lies there in the coffin. Here, funerals are viewed as a part of social life. I find this acceptance a great relief, especially as in the West many find the thought of death a discomforting topic to be avoided.

Gently, I pull the buff-coloured boots on to Vic's lifeless feet. She had painted her toenails aqua blue the week before, a colour I thought strange at the time. I assumed it was a teen trend, but now I see it as a morbid blue, befitting the icy tinge of Vic's bloodless skin. Her lips are white, too, with the life drained out of them. Her skin is the palest I've ever seen. It is strange to see Vic's face so unmasked. She never went anywhere without make-up. Sharyn and Paula, more skilled than I, lovingly put eyeshadow on closed lids, add pink blusher to cheeks, a rose tint to those white lips.

We decide what to put in the coffin with Victoria. I feel a visceral need to do this, but it is also part of the Chinese approach to the ritual of death: objects are put in the coffin in the belief the deceased might have need of them in the afterworld. I put in beloved soft toys from childhood, her favourite pyjamas, and photos of family to be with her forever. She was never without jewellery, and I place a large turquoise ring on her finger and jangling bracelets on her arms. I miss the jangling. The Chinese also like to give the loved one food to take, signifying the continuing relationship and interdependence among a family even in death. A colleague and neighbour, Pat Wee, goes to Victoria's favourite bakery on our road, Balmoral Bakery, and orders special food to tide our daughter over on this most unwanted and unexpected of journeys. Even though his shop is closed on Good Friday, the owner bakes a box of egg tarts, always Victoria's treat of choice amid shelves of tempting eclairs and curry puffs.

Malcolm taps my shoulder. "It's time," he says, trying to stay upright but trembling. Then he leans forward and kisses our child's forehead one last time. I lift her fingers, trying to retain a memory of their gentle feel, the beauty of their length, how they stroked the fur of our cats, how they touched my cheek.

We cast rose petals on her body. They are pink tears dotting her with love. Then the coffin lid is closed with a soft thud. I want to run to the coffin and scream and lose myself as I cling to what remains of my child. But I hang on to what might be dignity, if not for myself or Victoria or Malcolm then for the mourners with us.

Someone places a bouquet of pink and white flowers on the lid of the coffin. The colours indicate the deceased is female and a child. Several strangers, employees of the funeral home, dressed in white shirts, black vests and black ties, carry our daughter on her white palanquin to a white hearse with glass sides. The glass enables passers-by in the street to observe the coffin on its journey. This is a common sight in Southeast Asia, although it would be unheard of in New Zealand.

On the bonnet, a huge bouquet of flowers has been fastened. And beside the driver, in the passenger seat, we are surprised—but somehow pleased—to see a large photo of Victoria, framed with three rows of tiny yellow roses. It is a photo of her in happier days, looking radiant and wearing an old school uniform: a soft white shirt and twill skirt. She looks much more relaxed in it than in the new school uniform she ended up wearing for just two months and two weeks, a demure dress with prim white cuffs that she said made her look like a flight attendant.

Vic's face beams from the passenger seat, seemingly excited and amused to be sitting high up and about to travel the bustling city streets of Singapore, then on to a highway leading to more green parts of the island, to the crematorium at Mandai, close to the zoo she used to visit as a child.

Malcolm and I stand behind the hearse. We hold hands and gaze with disbelief as the doors close on our dead daughter. This cannot be us. This is not happening. I should be with her. She can't leave us. But the three days of the wake have helped us accept this next stage. Pink, white and yellow flowers line the hearse's windows, imparting a strangely joyous effect.

I hear a pattering sound and realise Malcolm is now holding an umbrella someone has given him. It's raining. The patters tap out the urgency of departure. The hearse's engine is running. I am enfolded by drifting dampness. The rain is fitting. I am too numb to weep, but the heavens do it for me. Such is the sadness over your death, Victoria.

A cortège has formed behind us. The tradition used to be that family members would walk all the way to the graveyard, but here, in modern Singapore, mourners line up as a final mark of farewell before getting into cars or buses to go to the crematorium. We have only Sharyn and Paula with us as family, but Fiona lines up too, and colleagues join the solemn procession, many clutching blue umbrellas handed out by the funeral company. We all walk forward a few steps as the hearse pulls away. Then it is lost amid rain and traffic. My last glimpse is of the bouquet of white and yellow flowers on the bonnet, as if it were a wedding car taking a young woman to a chapel to get married.

9

MONKS CHANTING

The funeral service has distanced Victoria from Malcolm and me in an unexpected way. Our daughter has become public property, on view in her white coffin in the centre of the crematorium chapel. We have lost the intimacy of the Sapphire Room, which we had turned into a de facto living room with photos from home, stuffed toys, albums of memories, and food and cups of tea and coffee.

Victoria, up there alone, faced by rows of pews, has become a distant object, one that can be judged, mourned or ignored. I am not prepared for this. I go up to her and whisper that Mum and Dad are still here, don't worry. We're in the row at the front. Music starts, people file in, and I find an order-of-service programme in my hands. It's a list of songs and speakers, with the service led by Pastor Chua Chung Kai of Singapore's Covenant Evangelical Free Church, who, it turns out, is known not just by two sets of Singapore neighbours but by Malcolm's friend, photojournalist Terence Tan. A week ago, if I'd been told that a pastor from an evangelical church would be playing a major part in our unholy lives and leading us in prayer, I would have laughed and cried out, "Praise the Lord and pass the bullshit detector." Yet here we are, and grateful he has taken us under his wing.

Somehow, Pastor Kai, as everyone fondly calls him—without previously knowing us or Victoria, and having had to deal with us in our incoherent state of shock—has put together a programme sheet, complete with lyrics. The hymns are simple enduring ones such as "The Lord Is My Shepherd" and the service closes with "Amazing Grace". A pop song Victoria is said to have liked is to be played—"Keep Holding On" by Avril Lavigne. I had no idea it was her favourite and don't even know the tune. Perhaps one of her friends had suggested it.

I can barely put thoughts together, let alone make sense of things. It does occur to me, though, that Malcolm and I are not down to speak at our daughter's funeral. Pastor Kai probably asked us but I can't remember. Is it a "bad Mum" thing not to farewell your own child at her funeral, not to stand up holding back the tears and display the depth of your love to the nodding approval of the congregation? But perhaps it is best that I don't—both Malcolm and I are heavily sedated. It's the only way we can get through this day. If I even made it to the lectern to speak, my words would probably choke in my throat, or worse, emerge slurred, as if I were drunk.

I see that the ushers are prefects from Victoria's school. Many of our Singapore friends wouldn't have known the full nature of the expat politics at play. It's all about protecting the school brand. Most international schools in Singapore are for-profit private ones and charge hefty fees. The nature of Victoria's death—suicide—might put off "customers".

I notice with a sickening horror that the prefects are kids Victoria loathed. They are the high-achieving, well-connected, popular ones. I remember that one of Vic's favourite tunes, which even I, the out-of-touch Mum, was aware of, was "Pumped Up Kicks", an edgy pop number about a troubled lonely youth who is not one of the cool kids and wants to shoot his fellow students.

Someone in the school hierarchy has made the prefects wear their starchy school uniforms, even though it's a public holiday. Was it perhaps the rising-star teacher of the upper school, who is fluttering about like a prima donna and is listed in the programme as giving a speech? She is dressed in flamboyant style with a red dress and scarf and dramatic make-up, as if she is to go on stage at a theatre and perform. I avert my eyes.

But there is a glimpse of sanity. In another pew I see a knot of girls, some in glasses, who look deeply sad and who I assume are Victoria's genuine friends. I did not get to meet her circle as we lived far from them.

No one from this group, nor any of the prefects or teachers, greets us. Mercifully, newspaper colleagues and neighbours come and embrace us and share our sorrow.

Pastor Kai, a remarkably empathetic man who came to his religious calling after a background in science, conducts the service with dignity; his words are heartfelt. After that, the teacher in red and another speaker from the school praise the school and its students and staff, and hardly mention Victoria. I may be realising there were sides to Victoria I did not know, but they didn't know her at all.

Malcolm and I now stand next to the coffin, handing out single white flowers—lilies?—to mourners, for them to place in the coffin as they line up and file past. I don't know who arranged this. I suppose it is well meant. Perhaps it makes the mourners feel they have put a bit of themselves inside that box of grief. And then there's the symbolism of the flower, with its white for purity, innocence, not quite adult. I am reminded of corsages, flowers you pin on a dress or a lapel when a young person heads off hopefully and excitedly on a rite of passage such as a school formal. And here we have the prone cold body of a teenager who will be forever seventeen, who never even got to sit her final exams, let alone go out into the world. I can understand the idea of the flower, but if it had been up to a more conscious, non-sedated me I would have handed out sprigs of lavender, one of Vic's favourite flowers. Or snippets of pink, purple and white bougainvillea from the pots that grow on our balcony, tended by Vic herself over many years, through the unseasonal drought that persisted for months before her death. Lavender and bougainvillea are not so redolent of corsages and funerals.

Standing with Malcolm shaking hands with mourners, it feels as if I am concluding a soirée and seeing guests off at the door. If I could speak even semi-coherently, I would be saying, *Thank you for coming. Did you have a nice time? Sorry about the lack of food. I'm sure you understand. What did you think of the entertainment? See you next time.*

The service has gone over the allotted forty-five minutes and the mourners for the next funeral are impatient to be seated. The chapel at Mandai Crematorium is managed by the Singapore government through its National Environment Agency. The crematorium marks the final journey on Earth for most Singaporeans. We are just one of several services scheduled at the four service halls, as they are called. We are in hall three. Three is a good number, I think, better than being in hall four, which is regarded by the Chinese as inauspicious as it sounds like the word for death in Mandarin. But what am I thinking? She *is* dead.

Next up at our hall three is a Buddhist funeral. Monks start chanting as Malcolm and I still stand, tearful and in shock, as hands clutching white flowers keep advancing to the coffin. The chanting gets louder. At the edge of my vision, figures in saffron robes are now dancing and banging drums. Outside, an open-back truck passes with a load of white-clad musicians from a Chinese ensemble, blowing trumpets out of tune and clanging on cymbals, on their way to drop off another coffin. The noisy racket is believed to drive away evil spirits.

This confluence of cultures is more Victoria's style. This is the all-embracing, spontaneous, tolerant Singapore she knew and loved. The impatient monks and the ramshackle band are more fitting for her send-off than the school prefects, for whom she is probably just a source of curious remorse.

We realise most people have gone. The coffin and Victoria are being wheeled away to a furnace, one of several roaring, glowing cremators, as they are called. There is even a place where mourners can watch the casket glide on an automatic pulley system into the depths of its burning heart. I think someone asks us to go and watch. Do we wish to put ourselves through that awful sight? Although I don't think I consciously know what they mean by "viewing area", I shake my head.

My next memory is of being in a swirl of mourners in the lobby of the "waiting hall". People hover, not knowing what to say. I notice with bitter satisfaction that one of the uniformed prefects is in a corner, in tears and utterly distraught. She and Vic had been friends briefly, years before. Vic was thrilled by the friendship as this girl was one of the popular, outgoing, pretty ones. They went horse-riding together and Vic, in her sweet innocence of the fickle nature of schoolgirl friendships, thought she had found her Best Friend Forever. However, the girl had suddenly dumped her for someone else. Vic was devastated. I felt guilty and blamed myself and Malcolm: perhaps we behind-the-scenes media types weren't dynamic and wealthy enough for the expat kids at this international school? The girl's parents ran their own business, were confident, outspoken and made the most of social occasions and networking. Malcolm and I liked reading books, discussing the news and living quietly. Poor Victoria. But, regardless of the environment, girls around that age of ten are flighty with their friendships. They are finding out who they are as people and who they like to hang out with. They can be unintentionally cruel as they casually discard friends, acquire new ones and enter different social groups.

I am appalled that I am finding satisfaction in the prefect crying in a corner. I am not someone who usually thinks like that. But here I am, thinking, "You made Vic suffer. Now you know what it's like."

Girls who are Victoria's real friends approach us. They are cautious when I want a group hug. I will learn later that they were advised by the school not to speak to me. I fight to hold back tears in order to allow some space outside my own mourning to consider what these girls might be feeling, what the loss of Victoria means to them, and also simply to memorise their faces as I have met them only once or twice before. One of them, Hannah, is especially uplifting. She has a warm open face and answers my questions with a graceful intelligence. Why would you take your own life when you had a friend like Hannah? Another girl is a downward-eyed closed book, yet waves of grief come off her as she lingers at the edge of our group. She is a slight girl, bland even. Her mother, whom I have not met before, comes over. She is blonde and helmet-haired, with the kind of corporate face I flinch from. She tells me her daughter, Mary, was a close friend of Victoria. I never knew. I am trying to take this in when she invites us to visit her home a few nights later, saying cryptically, "It will give you one piece of the puzzle, but it won't give you all the answers." All I can do is nod. I don't know what she means.

Our apartment, after the second worst day of our lives, is a sanctuary. Malcolm's buddies from the Singapore photography scene are here, making sure we are not alone. There's big-sized, big-hearted Bryan van der Beek, who has the gift of keeping things moving along with an easy laugh. There's Terence Tan, a gentle presence. The inimitable Tay Kay Chin is there with quiet wisdom in his world-weary eyes. Young photographers—"the kids" as Malcolm calls them—sit around cross-legged, checking their phones, playing jenga or checking their cameras and peering at lenses. They have been going to wakes since they were children and know the routine.

They are a restless, chattering presence, but respectful of our grief. The media world in Singapore is a small one. Carl Skadian, editor of *Today*, a rival newspaper to *The Straits Times*, is a constant, welcome presence. He's been with us since it all began. *The Straits Times*' travel editor, Amy Lee, is another visitor. Stephanie Yeow, the newspaper's picture editor and Malcolm's boss, brings steaming soup from a hawker centre. Later, she sits on the edge of the sofa and takes photos. Taking photos is a reflexive act for these people. They're not avoiding the reality of grief by hiding behind a lens; they're documenting it so we can perhaps make some sense of it. It is a comfort to have them here, even though I don't know them well. Fiona, my friend from my hometown, Auckland, chats easily to these strangers like the experienced general practitioner she is. I am grateful for that.

Gradually, though, people filter away. I go out on the balcony where the sky is black velvet and the stars are dots of distant fire. It is still a time of drought. There are no piles of monsoon storm clouds puffing up to take over the sky. The only sound is someone trying repeatedly to kick-start a motorbike. It's a clank, a cough, and a small roar that dies away. I peer over the balcony edge and see Bryan van der Beek helping Terence push his dead bike. Tyres softly scrape the asphalt and there is a faint squeaking of wheels. A carpark security light captures the two leather-clad men either side of the bike. I feel bad that their night has ended this way. And I feel unbearably sad. Something of me is dead and is being pushed into the darkness, too.

10

NOT ASH

Two days later, Malcolm and I enter a small side room off the lobby of the Singapore Casket Company. It's on a different floor to the one for the three-day wake. Unlike that room, this one has windows. Sun streams in. An Indian man, wearing overalls, stands next to a plastic bag that's on a table. Seeing us, he looks startled. The funeral parlour does not get many Westerners taking up one of its traditional Chinese-style funeral and cremation packages.

He squares his shoulders and beckons us with dignity. He nods to a box next to the plastic bag. The colour of the box is the audacious orange of a Hermès wrapping, as if it contains some overpriced frippery. However, it contains the marble urn we ordered yesterday for $162. Francis helped us select it. "Go for middle-range. Too expensive is a waste of money," he had advised, his migrant-descendant frugality an offering of love. We, novices at this business and with family in another country, had been grateful for his help.

The cremation package we chose included the

category "ash collection". The man in overalls is a worker from the cremation centre where the funeral was held. We realise this now, observing his practised proficiency. He removes the urn from the box and places it next to the plastic bag, which he opens. I notice that the bag sits with a certain formality on a raised plate with fiddly silver legs. The formality and the fiddly legs remind me of doilies on Grandma Sheila's chintz sofa. We are handed metal tongs. Why would you need tongs for ashes?

There's a rustle as the bag is opened, and then a rattle. I prepare for a choking swirl, or perhaps a floating essence that rises to dance in the sunlight.

Instead, there are chunks of bones.

We should have ticked "Grinding" in the cremation package list. I told you we were new to this business.

For Malcolm, it is yet another cruelty. He falls into a chair. He buries his head. He is angry. His daughter has been mutilated. Fine dust, he could accept. Not this. He is saying, "No, no, no."

The cremation worker glances awkwardly from angry man to smiling woman. Yes, I am smiling. Because these remains are so clearly her.

I reach into the bag. The man opens it wider for me. He smiles tentatively, reverently. I pull out the bones of a complete index finger. The day before, dressing Victoria for her last journey, I had placed a huge turquoise ring on it. The cheap keepsake my seventeen-year-old so adored has protected the finger from the fierceness of the fire.

From my purse I pull out a yellow gold ring. I bought it

for her when she was a toddler, for good luck. Something told me to bring it today. I gently slip it over those three small curved fine bones that, even now, form a point.

My husband is white-faced with anger as he sees me delve into the bones, caressing the curves and twists. A knot of spinal column. A tiny bit of a pelvis that will never bear children. The remains of toe bones.

The nails had been painted corpse blue. Now I know why Victoria chose that colour at the beauty parlour the previous week. Today, all pieces of her are purest white, tinged with the pink of the tropical sunsets that she loved. Yet, after the blast heat, they could be the fossil remains of an ancient creature, not the bones of someone alive just six days ago.

Our keeper of the plastic bag wields his own tongs, sorting the bones and placing them inside the urn. He places some aside that, at the end of his procedure, he puts on top. I gasp. They are from her skull. There is her browbone. All mothers know the contours of their child's forehead. They place their hands on it to soothe a fever, banish a bad dream. Even when she was older, a teenager, I would slip into her room when she was asleep, kiss that brow and whisper, "Mummy loves you."

I touch this curve of a mother's heart, my heart. Malcolm stands, leans on me. The cremation worker puts the urn in the orange box, fastens atop it a matching cardboard lid, lifts the heavy load and hands it to us.

"Your daughter," he says.

11

THINGS INSIDE

We return to our apartment. Malcolm has the orange box tucked under his arm. His sisters Paula and Sharyn are still here, thank goodness. Their living physical presence is a sharp reminder of Vic. The aunts and their niece shared a similar beauty. They have the same blue-grey eyes, soft peachy skin and elegant, long-fingered hands. Sharyn, with the natural authority of the eldest sibling, takes the box from Malcolm, removes the urn and without any forethought reaches up and places it on top of a tall egg-yellow chinoiserie cabinet in the living room.

She pauses to assess the placement and then nods, the strands of her chic brown hair moving in unison, and turns to us for approval. The cabinet, which smells of camphor to keep the moths away, is where we store our linen. Cotton sheets and duvet covers for Vic's bed lie on its shelves. They are folded neatly, testament to an orderly mind. It was Victoria who had folded them. She was obsessive about getting the corners and edges matching. I am inclined to get bored with chores and shove the sheets in any old how. "Mu-um," she would say.

The cupboard is decorated with paintings of vaguely outlined blue and red butterflies. They look elegant and floaty. It is a very "Vic" decoration. It is a far more fitting repository for her cremated remains than the alternative, I concede. This is the lowboy dresser, dominated by a TV that broods in its own vortex of blankness. So, atop the butterfly linen cabinet the urn will stay.

I nod, as do Malcolm and Paula. But I don't feel that the Victoria I knew is actually inside that urn at all. All her energy can't have been reduced to that, so right now it's of little significance to me where it sits. The feeling of being around the moving, laughing, fluid knot of Paula, Sharyn and Malcolm, with their shared DNA of Victoria, is enfolding me, lifting me. I reach out to hold it.

The two cats, Angie and Mittens, emerge from their hiding places and curl themselves around our legs. Both of them yowl. I assume they want feeding, or attention. All the years I have owned cats I have never bothered to watch them and listen to them, to learn how they communicate. The next morning, when I get up and open my bedroom door, they are sitting, patiently waiting. They look up at me, and then at an object they have placed directly in my path. I bend down.

It is a bone.

The bone is the length of a finger, quite old and

worn, and hollow in the middle. One of the cats must have got it from outside at some point—probably Angie, a lithe little black panther of a hunter—sneaked it inside and buried it in the soil of a pot plant.

And now they have hauled it out and want very much for me to see it. For me to understand that they understand.

What is in the urn.

Who is in the urn.

Malcolm and I go to the home of Vic's friend Mary, whose mother, at the funeral, had invited us to visit, with the cryptic reference to "a piece of the puzzle".

One puzzle for us is why they want us to visit. As far as we know, Mary was just one of Victoria's several friends. They had the odd sleepover, always at Mary's place. Vic mentioned Mary only now and then. She did not seem to be a special friend.

We get a taxi to the complex of upmarket, multistorey townhouses where Mary and her mother and stepfather live. It is night, and because we can't see the house numbers clearly we get lost. The place is designed for people who arrive by car directly into the underground parking area. For people who come by taxi and are dropped off, finding the street-level entrance is confusing. The houses are terraced in a tight community behind high fences and dense shrubbery. Malcolm strides on ahead, to what he thinks might be Mary's house, going by the few houses that have numbers. I follow and see him pause, staring into a living-room window. He turns, and gestures for me to be silent, and to come beside him.

We see the thin slight frame of Mary. She is next to her mother, who is on the sofa. Her mother sits upright, tense and anxious. Her blonde hair is still neat in its bob, but Mary is gently running her hands through its strands, over and over. She smooths the hair back with the kindest of strokes. The mother remains tense, upright. Mary repeats her soothing gesture, the stroking of her mother's hair. It is a touching, intimate moment, yet disturbing to witness. Shouldn't it be the other way around?

Malcolm and I step back, look at each other, raise our eyebrows. We wait a few minutes, then pretend we are just arriving, stomping up the steps, knocking loudly on the front door. The mother answers, looking totally composed. She gestures for us to come in but doesn't ask us to sit down. We wait, seeking a cue from her. Will there be a direct comment about the fact that Victoria is dead, some expression of sorrow, a revelation, even, of some aspect of why our daughter took her life? Instead, what follows is a bewildering tour of the house and compound, as if this is in itself the telling of an important story.

The terrace house is on four levels. A Filipina domestic helper apparently lives on the bottom level, but she doesn't make an appearance. The mother just points at the closed door to her bedroom. A sing-song voice calls out from within, "Hello."

I want to speak to the helper. If Victoria were here, she would have wanted us to speak to the voice behind the door, for the door to open, for there to be an embrace, acknowledging the universality of human loss. She wasn't into the cringe-making division where the hired help are treated like servants. She would have wanted to get to know the helper, find out her name, ask if she had children back home in the Philippines.

Later I will wonder if the helper had been instructed not to come out. Had Vic made a connection with her? Had secrets been shared? However, amid this hovering moment of uncertainty we are bustled up the carpeted stairs, to the living room and kitchen, and even given a peek of the laundry. We turn back into the open-plan living room-kitchen and linger awkwardly by the shiny white island bench. Mary tells us that she and Vic would make snacks here. "Vic taught me to make nachos," she volunteers.

"They did a lot of stuff here, fixed their own food," muses the mother, vaguely. Vic would have indeed loved the area, I think. It is sleek and modern, with lots of white.

We are led up to the next level, which has bedrooms and an ensuite bathroom and is the domain of the mother and stepfather. We climb a narrow staircase to Mary's bedroom at the very top. It is small but self-contained, with its own bathroom and deck. We are told that on sleepovers Victoria would be on a mattress on the floor. That she and Mary would talk for ages. That

Vic especially loved the wooden deck and lying out on it at night with Mary, staring at the stars.

They would lie there for hours, talking. "Vic knew so much about the stars; she taught me their names," Mary says. Malcolm and I look up. We see stars above, and in front of us an elevated view of a wealthy part of Singapore, houses on their own pieces of land, none more than four storeys high. There is not a public housing tower block to be seen, not even distantly on the horizon. Yet eighty percent of Singaporeans live in tower blocks on this island, which is about two-thirds the size of New York City. Victoria was conceived in a public housing flat barely two kilometres from here. It may as well be a hundred miles from Mary's small universe.

We go back down to the living room where, we're told, Vic and Mary would hang out, watching TV. The movie *Frozen* was a favourite, Mary tells us. Here, the tour of the house stalls awkwardly. Mary and her mother hover around the sofas. I sit down. Vic would have sat here, I find myself thinking.

I ask Mary if she has any more memories to share. Mary thinks for a while, then smiles and becomes animated as she relates how Vic loved swimming, whereas she, Mary, was nervous. In fact, Vic told her what to do if caught in a rip at the beach—not to fight the current, but to go with it until you got to the edge and out of its clutches. The knowledge had saved Mary's life when she was swimming with her stepdad at Phuket and they had got caught in a rip. Mary remembered what Vic had said and they were able to swim free of it. The stepfather had been "useless", Mary added. We don't know what to make of that comment. I end up nodding sympathetically, as if the uselessness of stepfathers were a universal truth.

Mary changes the subject, saying we must see "our" (hers and Victoria's) hang-out spot—the gym. We duly troop to the basement carpark. The gym is small, with mirrors around the side, a collection of weights and some treadmills. We are puzzled as to why Vic would like this spot as she preferred outdoor exercise such as cycling, walking and tennis. Besides, this place is dark, and its out-of-the-way location in a basement gives me the creeps. It is a grim place to toil away keeping fit. But Mary laughs incredulously. She says they didn't come here to exercise. It was where they could be alone and make as much noise as possible. They would sing at the top of their voices. They could talk for hours and no one would bother them. It was where they felt alive. "They were always in here," says the mother, in a tone that suggests she was pleased they were out of her helmeted hair.

The thought of my daughter in this depressing, isolated basement carpark cheering up her friend fills me with sadness—for both of them. They were teenagers with lives to live and fun to be had—going out, mixing with people, not contemplating the world and their confused inner selves from the confines of a breeze-block room that looks like a prison cell.

The walls close in. I feel as if I am choking. Despair seeps through the blockwork. Malcolm feels the same way; he tells them we will go now. Mary crumples. I want to hug her but I also want to shove her and scream, "Why are you the one alive?" I take a deep breath and try to grasp that this unassuming, secretive girl is grieving the loss of her friend, our daughter. Vic would have wanted me to console her. Some presence of mind or intuition had made me pick a piece of crystal from Vic's dressing table and bring it as a keepsake gift. Mary's eyes finally look at mine, with something that could be surprise and gratitude. She puts the crystal in the palm of her hand and caresses it. She thanks me and, averting her eyes, clutches it tightly.

We make our way past cars, up the concrete ramp to the road, not comforted at all, completely at a loss as to what Mary's mother had meant when she spoke to me at the funeral about a piece of the puzzle.

A few weeks later, we learn from the police that Mary could have saved Vic. Vic had tried to jump from the ledge early on Sunday morning, the day before she actually did so. For some reason she pulled back and texted Mary that she had nearly jumped. Mary apparently texted back that they would see the school counsellor on Monday. And something about making cupcakes. Mary never told anyone.

There was a whole 24 hours in which we could have saved her.

I wonder why Victoria reached out to Mary and none of her other, more confident, outgoing friends, who would have been alarmed by her text and contacted an adult. Did Mary tell her mother about Vic's text? I try to contact the mother. She does not reply.

12

SLEEPLESS

I remember that Sunday, our last day as an intact family. The knowledge that Victoria had already tried to kill herself now tarnishes every memory. I made her a cup of coffee that morning and she chattered away, seemingly happy, but now it turns out that just a few hours earlier she had been high up on an apartment building, willing herself to jump. After slipping back home, had she simply gone through the motions that day, with the determination that early the next morning she would finally commit to death? Or had she wavered, looking for a sign to keep living? I believe she had set herself a deadline to die. That she could not face another day of school. That the entire Sunday was a last goodbye. I relive every memory I can dredge up, agonising if there was a point at which I could have said something that would have changed her mind.

On that final Sunday before she died, Vic went out and bought presents for Mary at the mall, returning home to wrap them. She left them in a prominent place on her homework desk. One of the last things she said to me was to make sure Mary got those presents and a card that was beside them in a sealed envelope. They were for Mary's birthday, a week away, she said. In hindsight, it was an odd thing to say. But at that point I was thinking of the next day, of a new school term. I was also hungry. Vic had brought me back a kaya waffle-pancake from the mall. She knew I loved them. The coconut jammy sweetness was squished inside a soft waffle "sandwich", still warm. Vic knew me so well. "Toasted cheese sandwich to follow, Mum?" she asked. She did toasties the proper way, with the bread buttered on the outside, then sizzled in the frying pan.

"You not having one, Vic?" I asked.

"Nah, I had something to eat at the mall," she said. And I marvelled, "So you're making this just for me?"

"Yep," she replied.

Malcolm and I spend days and nights sitting on the sofa crying or else walking around the apartment. At first, we take sleeping pills and tranquillisers but they make us feel spacey and disconnected. We want to feel the pain of Victoria's loss, because at least it is something of her to feel. However, the result is that we don't sleep. The nearest thing to sleep I experience is blacking out, from which I emerge instantly awake, twitchy and unrefreshed. And always I wake with the knowledge that she is dead. There are no vestiges of dreams where she is alive. I don't seem to dream at all.

———

Two weeks after Vic's death, her school holds a memorial service. The teacher in charge of the choir which Vic belonged to gives a speech about how "she was strikingly tall and sang second soprano. Victoria gave one hundred percent to the ensemble. Over two years I don't recall her ever missing a rehearsal or being late."

There are eulogies that recall her beauty: "Her beautiful eyes, the fact that in every group photo she was always so photogenic. She couldn't take a bad selfie if she tried. The voice of an angel. The world was a much better place with her here." Her friends in the choir ensemble find the courage to perform the song "For Good" from the musical *Wicked*, which Vic had loved, and which has poignant lines about people coming into our lives for a reason with something we must learn.

13

ESCAPE

We need to keep moving. Or rather, we cannot keep still. Malcolm and I can't bear to be in our apartment. We can't bear to be in Singapore. We arrange for our neighbours Suan Choo and Mrs C Tan to look after our cats and we fly to New Zealand for two weeks. We fly, as in catch a plane, and we fly, as in make an escape. I need security, comfort, old friends. We head to Kakanui, our holiday cottage in the South Island.

For the first time, there are not three of us seated together in economy, although we have ended up in a row with the third seat spare. I take a window seat, the seat that was always Victoria's. She would get airsick and so flying was an ordeal. It helped a little if she could stare out at a horizon. For a mother like me, whose medical knowledge extended only to dealing with coughs and colds, Victoria's airsickness was a harrowing experience as I felt helpless. Victoria started vomiting continuously on flights from about the age of four. We tried having her avoid eating. We tried pills. I took her to a psychologist.

Nothing worked. Gradually Vic learnt to manage it, so by sixteen she could sometimes get through a long-haul flight without vomiting at all, although she would still feel nauseous. She would pull a blanket over her head and chew on peppermints and listen to music or read with the light of a torch, while taking occasional sniffs of the rescue remedy, peppermint or lavender essence that she had dabbed on her wrists. I'd bring plastic bags, wipes and spare clothing for her in my carry-on luggage. And I would avoid eating or drinking myself. Malcolm, in the aisle seat and anxious in his own way, would down whiskies like there was no tomorrow.

As I sit in Vic's usual seat, staring out the window, I remember being in her bedroom that last Sunday of her life, just twelve days ago. I was in a flurry of household chores and worried about getting her ready for the start of the new school term. She was strangely reflective, talking about things in her life over the years, as I bustled about her bedroom and she lay on her bed with a *Harry Potter* book. At one point, she said, "Mum, you know how I get sick on planes? It isn't what you think. It isn't anxiety. It's the smell of the food and the coffee. That's what makes me sick. It just makes me want to throw up. I'm all right up until then."

I remember being surprised she wanted me to know this right at that moment. I asked her what it was about those particular smells. I think she said they overwhelmed her and there was no escape.

Looking back, why did I not ask her more about it? Such as: "Why are you telling me this now? What are you really trying to say?"

Couldn't I see that this was odd, her giving me explanations about events in her life? Well, I could, but the "me" who was in "mother" mode—or at least, the mother mode that I thought society expected me to be in—was always looking to the future, wondering if Vic had done her homework, reminding myself to take the clothes out of the dryer and fold them, working out what to have for dinner. If only I had taken the time to stand back to take a proper look at her as she spoke. I recall now that she had been hunched over as she lay in bed with her book, and was very quiet, gentle and distant. In hindsight, she was already taking flight from us. And I could not see it.

I am still looking out of what I think of as her window. A cabin attendant asks me what meal I'd like for dinner. For the first time in fifteen years of flying, I order food and wine. Part of me wants to choke. Part of me is simply hungry.

As usual, Malcolm has brought along his noise-cancelling headphones and is already watching a movie while clutching a neat whisky—a single malt if he has been able to wrangle it. I don't begrudge him these simple pleasures. I know he is missing the person in the third seat, too. I try reading a gossip magazine but can't concentrate. Normally I would be focusing on

Victoria, wondering how she was feeling and fending off polite inquiries about her from the cabin crew. But now there is nothing for me to do. Except ache for her.

I turn to the inflight entertainment. No comedy or drama or thriller interests me. I'm not interested in fictional lives, or deaths. I call up a documentary, in the hope a factual story will be bearable. It is about the life of Helen Clark, the prime minister of New Zealand before she became a top-level administrator at the United Nations. I find myself caught up in watching the screen in a way I have never experienced before. Every emotion is intensified. Clark's early years on a farm move me deeply. Visits to relatives' farms when I was young are suddenly remembered. The patting of a calf when I was seven is as immediate as if it were happening now. I feel the so soft coat. The little black nose is so moist. The poo is so stinky.

The final scenes, when Clark's Labour Party loses a general election after nearly nine years in power and she appears on stage to make her concession speech, overwhelm me. It's not just Clark up there gripping the lectern, it's me. I concede defeat. I tried to do my best. I tried to be a good parent, a good role model. I tried to hold the family together. But it wasn't enough. Helen looks so brave and vulnerable and damaged, with a forced smile that resembles a snarl. And, channelling the defeat of this middle-aged female politician, my Proustian moments of recollection are not to do with the taste of dainty madeleine cakes but with smell.

The documentary cuts to the men of the victorious conservative National Party raising their arms in triumph and I smell their sweat-soaked shirts. It is a sour stench.

I tell myself to get a grip, to stop infusing this diversionary entertainment with my feelings of loss. This is just politics; it has nothing to do with Victoria's death and its aftermath. As for Helen Clark, I've never even met her. Glimpsed on TV, she always seemed a tough cookie, a sort of female patriarch with her blunt haircut and even blunter stare. Goodness knows why I'm suddenly assigning words like "vulnerable" and "damaged" to her. It would be laughable if I wasn't now sobbing and having to turn off the screen. Goodbye, dear Helen, whoever you are. Goodbye, Victoria. Sorry that Mummy couldn't help.

"Gee, that must have been some show," murmurs a passing flight attendant. I go into a toilet to wash the tears from my face. When I emerge, the cabin crew are busy getting dinner sorted. The odour as the tin foil is peeled away from the rectangular portions is a rush of stale air off something dead.

We land at Christchurch. There's a three-and-a-half-hour trip ahead. Malcolm drives. We don't stop at the café in the rural town of Ashburton, where the three of us would usually get out, wander around and have coffee and cakes. Just the sight of the café sign next to the supermarket carpark is painful. The routines of a family on the road are no longer for us.

Further on we pass coastal Timaru, yet another town whose fortunes ride on the cow's back, and which we used to enjoy mocking for its aspirations to be a tourist destination, a "riviera" of the south. The somewhat grim state highway runs through it. We would pass blocks of motel units proclaiming sea views of the much-vaunted Caroline Bay, yet rarely see anyone on the balconies. In a school essay, Victoria wrote: "There's nothing between here and the next town fifty miles away but dairy farms." Indeed, on the way to the next town, Waimate, the paddocks on either side of the highway are full of ruminating cows on grass made shockingly green by twenty-four-hour irrigator-fed water.

Soon the stench of freshly flayed flesh from the Pukeuri freezing works permeates the car. It's a reminder that we are finally on the home stretch. Once through Ōamaru's broad, tree-lined main street, we follow the coastal road to Kakanui, past waves tearing at cliffs, ragged patches of stony beach, potato fields made salty-rich by seaweed fertiliser, an honesty stall of fresh tomatoes for sale, and over an old, single-lane wooden bridge. We hurtle down a stony track saying "No entry" and up a muddy driveway to our cottage, on the side of a hill overgrown with gorse and unpruned fruit trees.

The old surge of excitement rises briefly. Friends have turned on the water and power and brushed the spiderwebs off the weatherboard cladding. We rush in, to feel Victoria's presence dancing in the sunlight and hear her laughter amid the breath of wind through grass left to grow too long. She is here.

And then she is gone. The sofas, windowsills and kitchen bench are beds of dust motes. Red and black lacquerware from Myanmar looks faded. A silver-coated bowl in the shape of a pumpkin, a Southeast Asian good-luck motif, is tarnished. Our house seems smaller, and the bedrooms are simply boxes. Even Victoria's. Malcolm had arranged for friends to take away Vic's bed from her bedroom. The sight of it would have broken our hearts anew. She'd had it since she was five years old. It was a fantasy Disney frame like something out of the movie *Bedknobs and Broomsticks*, white and gold with twirly bars. Back then, we would imagine it rising above the house, Vic clinging to the mattress and soaring over Earth, up to the stars.

I look in her room. I know the bed won't be there, but the shock of its absence is probably worse than if it had been. And there's something new I hadn't noticed before, that had been hidden by the bed—Vic had spilt purple nail polish on the carpet during the last Christmas holidays. She'd tried to wipe it off, but some has hardened in a distinct swipe. I will treasure this mark forever.

Later, when I go to hang the washing on a line strung under the carport, I notice a pile of cigarette stubs in the grass at the edge. They have been smoked, one after the other and quickly, as some are more half-burnt tubes than butts. It has been raining and I realise these are the cigarettes of a neighbour, dreadlocked, kind-hearted Matt, and his friends, who took the bed away. They have sheltered in the carport while having a smoke. I imagine them being upset, sucking the tar with shaking hands and, when the comfort didn't come, hurling them away one after the other, the paper and tobacco fizzling and dying in the grass.

That evening, the sound of rustling grass and leaves mocks the silence of the absent third person. I get Malcolm to turn on talkback radio, something I never normally listen to. He is horrified; he'd planned a different soundtrack to this journey. Obscure rock bands from the '70s, or concertos of heartbreaking virtuosity. Edgy country. Gram Parsons and Emmylou Harris. Absurd British humour. Peter Cook and Dudley Moore. But he obligingly turns the dial to angry people arguing about dole bludgers and when we will all be wiped out by a comet. He adjusts the sound level to a background murmur. As the whiny nasal tone of the radio host holds forth, I sit on the sofa for hours on end, through nights and days, wailing.

I don't remember much.

People come. Old friends Barbara and John get out of their car, hug us. Just a few months previously, on New Year's Day, they had taken Malcolm, Victoria and me to a funfair at Timaru. Today, four people look at each other in raw disbelief.

Barbara and I go inside. She sits next to me on the

rust-red sofa we brought from Singapore when Vic was young. We look out through the slider-door windows to the snow-tipped Kakanui mountains and the hinterland beyond. Privately educated Barbara, confident and practical, being of high-country farming stock, is not normally lost for words. She has counselled countless upset people in her job as a social worker. During the 2011 Christchurch earthquake she was in a building several storeys up with a client, a refugee from East Africa who was in a wheelchair. When the building stopped shaking, she somehow, by herself, got the terrified man down the emergency stairs to safety. Trying to cheer me up while missing Victoria herself—she and John, childless, always remembered Vic's birthday—she tries to find words of comfort. Victoria would have wanted me to be happy, she tells me.

She means well. It is a good thing to have said. However, I am unable to conceive of a notion such as happiness ever again. I don't want to seem ungrateful, though. Her visit is the stuff of true friendship and human decency. I attempt to smile through the tears. I'm at a loss as to what to do or say. I resort to the comfort of ritual. I make her a cup of tea. Earl Grey for a sense of decorum. And it was Victoria's favourite.

John and Malcolm are outside. John is a man of few words, most at home in old shorts and work boots tending to his vegetable garden. He and Malcolm go to the tool shed and get out an axe and a garden implement called a grubber. They spend the rest of the day hacking away at old man's beard, a climbing plant that is strangling the nectarine tree. It is a pointless task since the tree has never borne fruit in all the years we've owned the property. Much later I ask John why they tackled it. He thinks for a while. "It's typical of what blokes do," he sums up, gruffly but kindly. I guess he means that at times of unbearable emotion, men direct their feelings into physical action, preferably to do with the land. Unusually for John, he embellishes: "They'll stand and look at a piece of soil for ages." I find immense comfort in this image, in the stereotype of Man in Control, Taming Nature.

In the evening, I call my mother and father in Auckland. My mum is at first comforting as she expresses her shock and sadness. This is what I imagined. When everything turns awful, you can turn to good ol' Mum. I offer to fly her and Dad down to stay a couple of days. After a while, I realise she has changed the subject to my brother, and things his family are busy doing in their wonderful lives. She then talks about her sore knee, bad back, how expensive going to the doctor is.

I steer the conversation back to the prospect of her coming down. She doesn't seem enthusiastic. "It'll be expensive," she says, so I add that I will pay for the rental car.

"I've got to talk to your father," she says. The phone is muffled by a hand placed imprecisely over it, and I hear back and forth sighs and mumbling. Eventually it is Dad who comes on to the phone. "Yeah, well, it's not a good idea, Linda," he says bluntly. I know he dislikes flying so I say something like I would really like them to come down. "It's not a good idea," he repeats, adding after a pause, "It's your Mum." Both of us stay silent. "I see," I say, not really seeing. I have to assume he means well, but I think he's telegraphing that she might unload one of her outbursts on me and cause a scene if she came to stay.

I remember that last time we got together, two years ago, there had been awkward conversations. Mum would start to launch into a tirade about the laxness of the manager in charge of their retirement housing, or how ungrateful neighbours were for the help she gave them. I would feel she was really pointing to something remiss about me, her way of saying I had neglected her. I wished she could have expressed that, so I could have explained that I felt truly sorry but living in another country and with a child it was all very difficult.

Dad would catch her eye and shake his head and she would suddenly be quiet. She would bite her lip and launch into something else. The price of petrol. The successful daughters of her friend Betty. People she knew who had died. All safe topics. And while she chattered, Dad would watch her, nodding approvingly, or shaking his head slightly if she started to venture into the places she longed to go: her perception that I was obsessed with money (I worked on a financial news desk); her need for financial help; the attentiveness of my brother; the skateboarding, rugby and arts awards won by his two sons. By comparison, I neglected her, Malcolm was a free-spender and Victoria was hoity-toity. This was probably a refrain experienced by many of the Kiwi diaspora living different and seemingly more privileged lives overseas.

Dad's voice falters as he says goodbye. He is choking down his grief to protect Mum, I know. He loves her deeply. I accept that he is incapable of expressing his feelings. I would be incapable of even saying the right thing, should he ever do so. And lurking deep down is the knowledge that he has been here himself. When I was about five, his father—my grandfather—had cancer and took his own life by walking into the sea. Dad found his body under a jetty. What would it have been like to experience that tragedy? And then to try and live, to go on raising a family, with those images haunting you?

One night Malcolm and I go to the boatsheds at the mouth of the Kakanui River and light a fire for Victoria. The making of the fire has been a ritual observed over the years by Malcolm and Victoria. Every holiday they would drag driftwood to a spot among the stones on the estuary edge and set it alight. Sometimes Malcolm would bring a skillet and cook sausages over the flames, or they would toast marshmallows on sticks. Vic would lug a basket containing Diet Coke and plastic glasses, even paper napkins. She loved picnics of any description.

Once the fire was going, at that point at dusk when the water was still, Malcolm and Vic would search for stones to skip. It was an art form for them, to spin a stone skimming and dancing across the flat surface. They could do it for hours.

Malcolm's friends from the area—some from clans whose ancestral roots go back to ancient Celtic times, others who trace their roots to canoe migrations across the Pacific—gather around the fire. People hug me. I can't hug them back. The fire upsets me. I associate it with the cremation, with unbearable thoughts.

And I am reminded of the last fire here when we were all alive. It was New Year's Eve, nearly four months ago. I remember I felt a sense of foreboding and was depressed, although I didn't know why. Perhaps I'd been thinking this would be Vic's last year of school, our last year as a family before she left for tertiary study. I had not been able to face the ritual of the fire at the estuary. Vic and Malcolm had begged me to go with them, but I'd fobbed them off, saying I was tired. They set off happily enough. At midnight I sat at my bedroom window and stared across at the dark valley. Only a streetlamp at the intersection of the main road and the turn-off to Kakanui illuminated the blackness. Then I heard yells and cheers from isolated pockets of revellers at the boatsheds, and from sand dunes at the nearby ocean beach, and from the grassy knolls in the uplands. The wind caught their voices and carried them to me as voices have carried in these parts ever since humans gathered around fire, be they Māori or Caucasian, sealers or whalers or newly arrived settlers. Fireworks erupted into the sky. The feeling of dread about the year ahead increased within me. I stared out the window, tears running down my face, as my phone lit up with Happy New Year texts.

Now, friends and neighbours come to the fire we have lit in honour of Victoria, giving looks of encouragement, raising a glass of wine or a bottle of beer as a type of salute, asking how I am. I try to be the rock they hope for. People can take only so much distress and hair-tearing. They need to be given to, as well as to give. What they want from me is hope that I can carry on, that everything will be sort of all right. I have to draw such a response from very deep within me, but I can be composed for only so long and leave the group. Flowing-haired Rhonda, our neighbour, lover of dogs, keeper of errant hens that nest in trees, and rescuer of all stray animals, says later she could tell I wanted to be alone or she would have joined me.

I go for a long walk to the nearby promontory, where blue penguins nest under a cliff and the occasional seal lumbers out of the sea to rest. The promontory is composed of ages-old lava rock, the once-molten outflowing of an ancient volcano that spilled all the way here and collided with the cold sea in a hissing roar. Now paua cling to the basalt crevices, along with thick strands of seaweed that resemble the unruly plaits of giants.

I stare out over a sea that stretches uninterrupted to South America and wonder where my Victoria is. Is she just cold ash and bone, or does she burn brightly as a spirit set free? Sparks from the fire at the boatsheds swirl past. The red dots of embers and ash spin out over the waves, flying to the horizon. I decide she is a spirit, free. I will keep her, all her energy, all her positive spirit, alive somehow.

I return to the fire. An older woman I know only slightly presses something into my hand. It's a small woven flax pouch with a piece of greenstone inside. A jade offering is regarded as a talisman by Māori.

"For you," she says.

I grip it hard, this gift. I look in her eyes and can see that she understands. She does not expect anything back. I learn later that her son had just been convicted of murder and she was going to move away, the sorrow was too great.

At the fire, she tells me only that she is going to another country to live.

The future, like the past, is another country.

LOSS

II

14

SHAKEN

Things had started to unravel nearly three years before Victoria died. Our housekeeper was suddenly sent back to the Philippines for alleged moonlighting. It's against the law in Singapore for domestic helpers to work for other employers outside your own household. Mae rang me at work sounding upset, something about the police or some uniformed officers having arrived at our house. She was to be taken away for investigation. Whatever the circumstances, I knew one thing: it was vital that Victoria, who had just become a teenager, could say a proper goodbye to her much-loved auntie, as she called Mae. I managed to call her at school and together we rushed home in a taxi.

Mae was sitting on her bed in her room by the kitchen. Two young officers in smart dark blue uniforms were hanging about at the back door, waiting for us to arrive.

Mae got up and threw herself into my arms. "I'm sorry, Ma'am," she said, using a form of address I'd always been uncomfortable with, but which in her culture carries a sense of respect, or perhaps a desired delineation of roles for both parties. We enfolded Victoria into our arms, crying.

There was nothing we could do at that moment about the legal accusation. The policemen were two guys, doing their job, but sympathetic. They agreed, and even shouldered her hastily packed suitcase.

Mae knelt and looked intently at Victoria. She reached out, held her by both shoulders and said, "Promise me you'll always be good for your mama and papa."

Victoria nodded deeply, and then Mae, in her skinny jeans and defiantly vertiginous high heels, was clattering down the steps of the apartment block behind the officers. Her lovely long black hair swished one last time in our view. We called out to her as she disappeared: "Love you! We'll visit you. Don't worry." And then Victoria shrieked, "Don't go." She went to run after Mae and I held her back. "No, no, no," she sobbed.

Out of the corner of my eye I noticed a domestic worker standing at a ground floor doorway, her arms folded, smirking. She had always been jealous of Mae, saying that we expat employers treated our domestic workers too leniently. Victoria saw her too. She broke off her crying and narrowed her eyes.

At the newspaper, we were changing over to a new computer system for editing and I found it difficult to use. I complained to one of the technicians, who mistook my exasperation for what he regarded as that of a typical high-handed foreigner. It was a time of much anti-foreigner sentiment; a looser employment policy and new higher population targets had resulted in a flood of migrant workers. Suddenly, Singapore had become crammed with new faces and the infrastructure was straining at the seams.

So, too, were tempers. A younger Singaporean colleague at work took against me, leaving a wreath of dead flowers on my desk and accusing me of being a "nobody", hired because of my husband. It ground me down. I am not the type of person to defend myself. I internalise things and blame myself. I took to going to the top of the Singapore Press Holdings building and wishing I could jump off. At home, I would suddenly burst into tears. Victoria would comfort me and tell jokes to cheer me up. But it made her sad, too. A sensitive soul absorbed my depression.

One day, the colleague put a sign on one of the desk dividers, with a Chinese symbol that had an angry destructive face, or so it seemed to me. It looked directly at my back. I felt uncomfortable. Perhaps it was harmless, but it seemed a provocative thing to do.

A few days later, on February 22, 2011, we were shaken to the core by a devastating event in our home country. An earthquake measuring 6.3 on the Richter scale hit Christchurch, where we owned a house. A total of 185 people died and over 6,000 were treated for injuries. More than 10,000 houses, including ours, were wrecked and had to be demolished.

Singaporeans were shocked by the news. Some had happy memories of holidays in New Zealand. About 116 servicemen of the Singapore Armed Forces, on exercises in New Zealand, were diverted to help staff cordons in the devastated city. The republic also sent a 55-member contingent from Singapore Civil Defence to assist in search and rescue operations.

I was not physically affected: I was living in Singapore and the house was rented out. The problem was the aftermath. Dealing with insurers and builders was stressful. The long, drawn-out process sucked away my time, my attention as a parent, my soul, my physical well-being. No one in Singapore, whether local or expat, cared much. The only people anywhere who did were, naturally, those affected in Christchurch. I joined a closed Facebook group of people sharing advice on dealing with insurers and builders.

The main problem was how to get back the equity in the house. I'd worked hard to buy it. You can't just walk away from NZ$600,000. My due as a policyholder was for a replacement house to be built, and the cash-only offers by insurers were insultingly low.

Due to complications thrown up by the insurer and builder, this was to take the next six years of my life.

I had not particularly wanted to buy the house but I'd had some funds available. Victoria had seen the house on the internet and fallen in love with it. It reminded her of the old colonial black-and-white houses that survive in leafy outposts around Singapore. So, rashly but after some due diligence, I bought it. It was seventy years old, a two-storey plaster and brick house built in a post-war Spanish mission style in the hills above Christchurch, an area with the exotically evocative name of Cashmere. (There is even a Bengal Road.)

While the house was not my style at all, fussy, feminine, and vaguely French country-style, part of me was drawn to it because a few doors down the road there was a house in a similar style that had been the home of the crime writer Ngaio Marsh, of whom I was a fan. Her house had become something of a shrine, visited by loyal fans and kept much as it would have been when she was alive. Unlike hers, however, ours was on a steep section. Its large garden, layered with terraces, contained hedges and plants that needed love and care. I am no gardener, but Victoria loved its nooks and crannies, places to sit and read a book in the sun.

There was a pragmatic reason, as well, for the purchase. Should our life in Singapore be affected by geopolitical events, Christchurch would provide a bolt hole. Singapore is a tiny island in a region subject to the ebb and flow of varying interests, internal and external. There was also the possibility of being kicked out through a domestic change of policy towards foreigners, or changes at our place of employment.

Meanwhile, I had rented the house to a family who had migrated from Sweden. Now it was broken, uninhabitable.

———

The thousands of people with damaged houses in Christchurch were looking to insurers to honour their policies. They needed their homes fixed or, if they were beyond repair, to have new ones built or be given financial compensation. My problem was that I knew nothing of my rights with the insurer, nor what building a house entailed. A home, yes. Bake some Nigella Lawson cinnamon muffins and let the waft of spice and sugar coat your family in comfort. You can build a home that way. But a house? Malcolm, a photographer and artist, knew how to make the concrete abstract, but dwangs and soffits? Where is the interplay of light and shadow in that?

After about two years the insurer agreed to build a replacement house. Victoria took an interest in the design and colours. She was good at things like that. Besides, she had happy memories of visiting the house during school holidays. We would call in on the way to our cottage in Kakanui after arriving in Christchurch from Singapore. The Swedish tenants included a sweet-natured blonde girl Vic's age. She and Vic would dash down to the garden and pluck the ripe fruit in summer. Eventually, they would return to us, giggling as they staggered up the slope to the house, wiping red on to their hands and arms from their berry-stained mouths.

For me, though, the visits were unsatisfactory. Our time was always fleeting. Malcolm would be anxious to get away down south, and property managers would be present, asking the tenants and us tedious questions about grout and peeling paint and tradesmen's access.

I liked the Swedish wife. Both of us disliked the property managers. We would slink off for furtive conversations while the inspection lists were ticked off.

"Is it nice to live here?" I once asked her.

"We love the house, but the neighbours look down on us," she replied. "Their children go to private schools. They tell me it is a Christchurch thing." I thought ruefully how this was replicated in Singapore, with the status-conscious mothers at Victoria's private school.

The Swedish woman asked if she could paint one of the bedrooms pink for the youngest daughter. Yes, of course, I said. The female property manager took me aside and told me tenants could not be trusted with paint. I knew I could trust the Swedish woman with anything.

In the earthquake the eldest daughter of the Swedish family would miss death by inches when the brick chimney on the house spun off and shattered on the garden where she was standing. She screamed as bricks fell into the berried hedges. She and the rest of the family fled the house.

15

STILL HALF A KID

Victoria is fourteen when the earthquake happens. She must have some idea about it, must notice before catching the school bus in the mornings that I am often on the phone to property managers and insurers in New Zealand. But she has worries of her own.

> I'm worried about Harry Potter ending, plus my childhood etc. [But] the actors will still be in other productions and you're anticipating Emma Watson's new movie which will come out soon. Just cos HP's finished does NOT mean your childhood has, too. You're still half a kid. And millions of other people are going through the same thing. With time the pain WILL heal.

This is a handwritten entry in a diary that has a hard cover illustrated with orange squiggles. It is among several diaries I find hidden under her bed after she dies. I had been with her when she bought it but hadn't realised that its purchase marked the beginning of extensive journaling, which would continue until two weeks before she died. Before that, she had small diaries and notebooks in which she jotted odd thoughts. But here, she starts firmly:

> Dear Diary. I hope I will be able to confide everything to you, not just notes and recounts, but my deepest doubts and secrets. I'll begin from the moment I bought you from the bookshop. It was a hot Saturday. Mum and I decided to go to the shopping mall (since there was nothing much to do). We always go straight to the bookshop to buy a book, or in Mum's case, the latest magazine. I picked up a few books and started reading them, but they were all boring chick-flicks. For some reason, I found myself wandering into the notebook and stationery section and found you.

She writes "in Mum's case, the latest magazine", which makes me wince as I love reading books. But dealing with the wrecked house in Christchurch, on top of running a household with Malcolm absent on weeknights, working on the newspaper, and me doing part-time editing work is wearing me out. Reading a gossip magazine takes me away from all that. Following the lives of celebrities is vacuous but reassuring. It's as if they are my substitute friends and family.

Dealing with the Christchurch issues is overwhelming. I know nothing about insurance replacement of a house, let alone the process of designing and building one. I can't even hammer a nail into a piece of wood. The multinational insurer and the large building company find our ignorance an advantage in negotiations. The insurer tells me that I am not allowed to know the value they put on the old house in terms of building a replacement. I take their word for it and sign a contract for a new house, unaware that it has been costed as cheaply as possible so I will get nothing like the quality of building and fittings I am entitled to. The insurers, or the builders, or the two in collusion, leave off vital parts of the construction in order to meet the low budget.

So while Victoria worries about outgrowing *Harry Potter* and starts to write about it, back in 2011 I am focusing on the new house. My thoughts telescope to the small world of insurance and building jargon. One of the engineering reports determines floor slope measurements for calculation of partial or full loss; gives geotechnical analysis of soil depth and quality; scopes the work; measures height planes; discusses existing use. An important term is "rebuild". That is what the insurer and their chosen builder call our replacement house. An entirely new house is to be built, but in their eyes they are rebuilding what we have lost. Perhaps that's why there is no excitement in the creation of this new structure. It is underpinned by disaster, for them and for me.

The language of the rebuild eludes me. It may as well be in Malay for all I can grasp. But if it were in Malay there would be a kindness to it, with declined nouns that invoked a sense of shared communities and values, and qualifiers that allowed for misunderstandings, acknowledging them to be perfectly natural and human, and more importantly, a mutually adjustable state of affairs. The language of the insurer is that of the corporate West, management-speak that hears only its own voice. It has meanings known only to the initiated and omissions deliberately designed to confuse. The language of the builder is exclusive. Dwangs, thermal-broken, rondo battens—terms such as these are potential minefields of extra expense if they are not examined, priced, queried, rolled around the tongue for size and spat out for effect.

What I forget to worry about is the new world that Victoria is entering, the one of adolescence: finding one's tribe, observing rites of passage such as periods, crushes and exams, entering social media friendships, finding a place for yourself.

A crucial event affects her deeply. Her best friend at the condo, Sivi, moves to Australia with her little sister, their dad, an Indian from Malaysia, and their Russian mother. Sivi and Vic have known each other for years. They are tall laughing beauties who travel confidently on public transport to malls to score free make-up sessions and go to Subway in the basement to eat salami sandwiches and hang out.

When Sivi leaves amid our tears, I still see Vic as this strutting weekend mall queen. I don't see that without Sivi she is lonely at the condo, and that at school she is falling behind her peers, and that she is not one of the cool kids. In one of her diaries, unknown to us at the time and shocking when we eventually read them, she writes neatly, in black pen:

> I want to commit suicide so bad. All the reasons are stupid and I have no dire reasons to kill myself like other people, like crippling debts, or no family, or physical disabilities. I feel really dumb and ashamed because I'm overreacting and I don't want to tell anyone because it's obvious they'll think I'm being stupid and I can work through and deal with my personal problems. I've started cutting my wrists and thighs with scissors and scraping skin with my nails. I already have 20 scars.
>
> I don't like cutting myself. It hurts, but it's becoming addictive. I feel like I'm temporarily destroying something inside me with the pain, and when I get sad or frustrated, I turn to self-harming. As soon as I start to scratch and the pain comes, I hear myself think "you have to do this, you're not worth anything." And I do feel a little better afterwards, and mainly it feels like the best way to cope with my problems and worries. ...
>
> You see, I'm in a sort of "clique" at my school; I belong with the other people in the sea of ninth graders who aren't technically popular. They are my friends, but I would feel more comfortable if they were my best friends. Or maybe I just want them to replace

Sivi. She was the one person I felt most comfortable being around with. She was practically the reason I got up every morning to face the day. She did have her own problems—one of them was feeling frustrated about being in Singapore. As she grew older, she became more and more irritated—I always thought that she fitted in at the local public school, where everyone is Chinese, Malay and Indian, and even though she looked Malay (on her father's side) she was still a Russian in her ways and in her heart. She wanted to feel free and go to a place where she belonged. And that was Australia. ...

All at once one day I saw her apartment empty. I felt like my childhood had been erased, and my friend was dead and not just moving to another country.

I never imagined that I would take her move so hard. Even though I hang out with my friends, sometimes it feels like I don't fit in. Or maybe I just want them to like me more, so that I can feel accepted.

As I read this, I wonder: why didn't Malcolm and I notice the scars? I remember asking about some marks on her inner wrist, but she said they were scratches from the cat.

It is at this time that Vic and her buddies become the target of the popular gang. And even within her group of friends, she feels marginalised. She develops social anxiety and is unable to answer questions teachers ask in class or participate in any way.

> I do seem to get left out and it seems like self-harm and not eating are the only ways they can notice me and value me, though I don't want to be thought of as an attention-seeker. People think that it doesn't bother me not speaking in class and being all "low profile", but it does. I feel that because of this, I'm not valued, and I tend to be self-conscious about the way I look, so I'm always worrying at school what others think of me—and I always assume the worst. Even just walking to class I feel embarrassed about the way I look, walk and talk.

As well as self-harming, Vic starts not eating. She finds this difficult, though, and tries vomiting up food, but it is difficult keeping the sounds from being heard. She's terrified of being found out. She starts to look for a more permanent solution:

> I've considered taking aspirin, but when I searched on the Internet, I found out it was a slow, painful way to die. I've considered drinking bleach, but it has the same effect. I'm just looking for a quick way to die. Several times, I've gone to the top floor of our condo, to get used to the height to jump off, but I'm afraid that by some miracle I'll survive but end up paralysing my legs for the rest of my life.

This is deeply disturbing to read. I tremble in anguish at such tremendous heartbreak within my own daughter.

To realise that your own flesh and blood suffered this way and had such dark thoughts is almost unbearable. How could we have been so blind? Why did Victoria not tell us? She must have wanted to, so many times. We would have wanted to help her. We could have saved her. How do you live with yourself, with the knowledge you saw her pain and did not save her?

At first, it was easiest to blame ourselves for everything. To loathe our ineptitude as parents, to hate our very selves. To sit yearning for our daughter, yearning to protect her and tell her you love her. The blame and the yearning are unbearable. You either kill yourself or find a way to keep going on.

One way was to consider other similar pain in our families. There had already been a suicide. Just before Christmas when I was five years old, my mum and dad had suddenly left my brother and me in the care of a relative and driven to the city, where my grandparents, Grandad Alan and Nana, lived in a sunny house next to a beach. When we next saw Nana, she was living in a tiny dark home in a basement, nowhere near the beach. We were told Grandad was "gone". Instead of Nana's usual smiles and hugs at seeing us, she collapsed on to the concrete stairs and lay face-down, sobbing.

No one in the family ever talked of what happened to Grandad Alan. It was something shameful. It was only when I grew up and got to better know a cousin, Alison, that I learned what had happened. Grandad

Alan had a brain tumour and a spreading skin cancer on his face. His death was what psychologists describe as "situational"—a sort of rational act to avoid further physical pain and suffering. He got up one morning, left a note for Nana, walked into the nearby estuary and let the current take him away. It was my dad who found the body. It had gone out with the tide, floated back and snagged underneath a jetty. It must have been horrible for my father, yet our family never spoke of it: the death, Dad finding the body, living with that, trying to go on.

Suicide messes with families, across generations. As psychologists tell it, a suicide can leave family and friends with unresolved emotional issues. Can obsessive thoughts about wanting to die be passed on genetically? Or is the seed planted when you are young and unformed, by a glimpse of sadness in your loved ones for which you blame yourself? Does the blame feed on itself?

My dad—Victoria's grandfather "Poppa Jim"—is forever waist-deep in the warm water of the harbour, holding his father's body.

16

HAUNTED

Looking back at that now distant country of the past, and needing to find a way through our failure as parents and all the blame we feel, a strange but welcomingly distracting thought occurs: Are our lives cursed? To Westerners such thoughts verge on superstition, even madness, but in Southeast Asia it is not strange to ponder these things. Many in that society are more open both to traditional religious notions of good and evil and to the ephemeral—ghosts, and good and bad spirits. Such beliefs are simply part of living and breathing.

Mae, for example, believed our flat was haunted. We had moved there around 2007 after losing our existing flat to "enbloc fever", a syndrome in which older condominiums are torn down for projects squeezing in higher numbers of apartments. There were few flats available for rent, so when this one came up I grabbed it. I recall Mae telling me the other maids thought there was a bad spirit here. I loftily dismissed the idea as mere superstition, although it is a dark flat and does not get much direct sunlight.

Doubts began to creep in when our toilets kept blocking and flooding. Plumber after plumber investigated. Eventually one found rocks and rags stuffed down a sewer. It seemed a previous inhabitant had done this deliberately.

Then there were the lightning strikes. Our flat has had more of these over ten years than we ever experienced elsewhere. We average at least one a year, despite having lightning conductors on the top of the building. Some strikes are direct: flames shoot out of the walls or leave scorch marks around plugs. These knock out the TV and computers and wi-fi.

Sometimes the boom of a lightning bolt hitting our balcony or a nearby roof adds to the terror. Once, Victoria was sitting at her computer and the hairs rose on her arms because there was so much static electricity in the air. She screamed as the sound waves hit her, creating a percussive shock. In a depressed mood, she wrote in a diary: "Or you can summon the coward's strength to ask the lightning to throw one last strike on to you, thus removing your selfish misery and despair for good."

At the top of the hill at the back of our apartment block, several mature trees are hit by lightning over the years. One tall straight tree catches alight and burns bright in the night, even in driving rain, like the blazing finger of God reprimanding us for our sins.

This hill is mostly parkland but on the other side of the condo boundary a sliver of jungle has somehow been preserved amid Singapore's rush to urbanisation.

By contrast, the condo section is a manicured domain. It has a tennis court, pathways for walkers, and a mixture of decorative shrubs and established trees. Every two weeks or so, maintenance crews cut the grass to keep insects, lizards and snakes at bay.

This hill has its own darkness. Before we moved there, a Japanese resident hung himself from one of the trees. A resident told me this in hushed tones when Victoria was a giggly three-year-old and we were at an outdoor puppet show right beside the tree, during an event to mark the Chinese Mid-Autumn Festival.

The path to the other side of the condo, to where Vic died, leads past the tree. Looming over the hillside is another ten-storey block, where an Indonesian domestic helper jumped to her death when Victoria was seven. We were on holiday in Kakanui at the time. Mae rang me from Singapore, telling me about the maid, and also that our beloved black cat Natalie had died, run over by a car the same day. The maids believed the spirit of the Indonesian woman had gone into Natalie. I was in a car with Victoria, just about to pull out of a driveway, and so she heard every word. The maids had put Natalie's body in a shoebox with white satin and said prayers over it. Mae was crying. I started crying, and when Victoria realised Natalie was dead, she said, "Oh no, Mum, no," and sobbed.

The morning that Vic died, she would have walked over the hill as insects chirped in the pre-dawn darkness, down an unlit path to the block, which is out of sight from where we live. Did she think of the Japanese man hanging there, twirling in a breeze off the hill? Did she think of the Indonesian helper and our crushed black cat?

Did the darkness scare her? Had she walked tentatively? Or was she racing to ascend to her secret spot while others slept? Was the sky illuminated by a blood-coloured moon? There was a lunar eclipse that night. Perhaps it was already unnaturally dark, the eclipse having pulled a switch?

Did she listen out for the rustlings and cries of predator and prey from the little patch of jungle? Or was it absolute silence she waited for, to either fling herself off to destroy her own body, or to slowly slip down, until she quietly dropped like ripe fruit?

During the last three months of Vic's life, little offerings to someone's gods began to dot the landscape. Sometimes, on a walk around the hill, I would find them left at the base of certain large trees that were believed to contain spirits, or to be spirits themselves. There were mandarin oranges and incense holders, sometimes candles. Once, I saw a whole pomfret fish, carefully lain on gnarled roots. Then, a more permanent fixture, a framed drawing of the toothy peaks of the famous Guilin limestone mountains in southern China, an emblem of nature's beauty, had been placed beside a tree along a walkway. Another time, that same drawing had been ripped out of its frame and thrown down a slope. The empty frame and broken glass lay haphazardly at the base of the tree.

It was at that time that rustling sounds began to be heard in the walls of the flat. I would be lying on my bed and hear whispers of tiny movements on a mass scale, as if the walls contained vast wads of tissue paper blown by a draught. One day, Malcolm and I were in the living room when the rustling started up. It became louder. A stream of long-bodied, translucent-winged insects flew out of skirting cracks. Hundreds, then thousands, filled the air until it was so thick the insects were crawling in our hair and falling down our necks into our clothes.

They were termites that had emerged from chewing through the wood holding up the walls and floors of the flat to fly out into the night and mate. Except they weren't flying out. With lights blazing in our living room, they were confused. I yelled for Victoria to close her bedroom door and stay inside.

The insects crashed into each other. Thousands of wrenched wings and separated bodies drifted to the floor. Under our feet there was a slippery silver pelt of wings.

Malcolm suddenly hit on the idea of turning off the lights and opening the doors to the balcony, where streetlights glowed in the distance. As one, the colony swooped out into the night towards the lights until every last one was gone.

This eruption, an almost biblical plague of insects, would happen once again in the three months before Vic's death. During those months, too, we sometimes awoke to mysterious early-morning chanting by monks in the flat above us, and the rhythmic playing of wind and percussion instruments. Incense drifted down. Once or twice there was a large metal incense carrier on the external stairway, with flames and smoke leaping from it.

I complained to the condo management about the flames, worried they were a fire hazard. Then there were problems right at our front entranceway. New neighbours moved in, immediately putting their kids' bikes and washing lines and knick-knacks and cardboard boxes in our part of the common area. They had an aggressive cat, which they left outside. It took to attacking our two cats, so we had to keep them permanently inside; before they would enjoy afternoon naps outside in the sun. The neighbour's cat learnt to balance on a beam separating the two flats and was able to enter our balcony and launch itself into our living room. We complained to the neighbours, who said it was our problem. We resorted to keeping the balcony doors permanently closed, making our flat even more dark, and us prisoners in our own home.

After Vic dies, I learn that the chanting and incense from the flat above were Taoist mourning rites for a neighbour who had passed away suddenly. I knew little of this neighbour, except that he was the father of two cheerful teenage boys and seemed a kindly man; he always gave me a smile when I saw him tending his potted plants in the common area. He had recently renovated his flat with new flooring and fresh paint, and had purchased Taoist jade statues, which he proudly displayed in his living room.

On Christmas Eve, getting up to admire the statues, he had slipped on the new marble floor and banged his head. He'd died shortly afterwards. The chanting and the processions of monks going over to the trees and carefully placing offerings at the base were rites aimed at returning order to the cosmos after the man's death. Where there is darkness, light must return as a balance.

I also learn later that some neighbours feel the spirit of the Taoist neighbour had "taken" Victoria as compensation, or for some spiritual hunger. I don't understand the complexities. The logical part of me says this is ridiculous. Another part of me is now open to the idea that there is indeed evil in the world.

Of course, it would be simplistic to think Vic took her life because of an external factor unrelated to her, to conveniently blame her death on an evil spirit that drove her to do it. However, perhaps there is some truth in the notion that something bad took hold of her way of thinking and made her fixate on negative things. She was such a kind, beautiful person that it is not inconceivable to think that for good there must be an opposite, evil.

At some point, soon after Vic's death, I see three Christian neighbours and a man I later discover is their pastor walking around the hill, saying prayers, and raising their palms high against "something out there", as one of them puts it. When I speak to neighbour Suan Choo she explains it was a prayer walk. "I was deeply troubled by Vic's death and the unexpected death of your neighbour," she says. "It was the second of two random deaths within such a short space of time and involving neighbours. I felt there was more to it and not coincidence. I spoke to a pastor's wife who said to gather fellow believers and do a prayer walk to cover and protect all the families there."

The pastor who conducted the prayer walk was Chua Chung Kai, the same man who had been contacted by a friend of ours, who does not know our neighbours, and asked to conduct Victoria's funeral service. Pastor Kai recalls to me much later being astonished when told the funeral was for Victoria McLeod. Was it the same girl, the young woman who took her life, he had asked. There are many pastors, vicars and priests in Singapore, yet it was this Pastor Kai—a man I had first glimpsed as a distant figure among a group of neighbours chanting prayers on the hill near where Victoria died—who was asked to conduct Victoria's funeral.

When Suan Choo and I are talking about Victoria, we get on to the subject of belief in the spirit world, something clearly apparent among many Singaporeans. She says, "Superstition has a lot to do with the unexplained, things that people can't make sense of, so they think it is something to do with spirituality and invoke pleasing the gods and ghosts. My son is doing his National Service in the army. I've learnt a lot from his observations of interacting with people outside his normal sphere.

"The army has a broad spectrum of people. My son goes to our church, but now he is encountering guys with tattoos all over their bodies and who keep apologising to the wall all night during Hungry Ghost Month [when it is believed the gates of hell open and the spirits are allowed to wander, even into army barracks]. These guys see spirits all over the place and to them it is perfectly normal.

"The thing is," she adds, "regardless of how we see the spirit world, it does exist and there are people who are more sensitive to it."

In the last two weeks of her life, during the school holidays, Victoria, who normally loved cycling and tennis, became a static, bed-bound person, with her earbuds permanently plugged in, listening to music—or possibly just as a barrier to conversation. When I went into her room, asking her to come with me shopping or anything to get outside, she would purse her lips, remove the buds reluctantly, and say, "What?"

Looking back, I should have yanked those earbuds out of her phone and hidden them for the rest of the school holidays. I shouldn't have nagged at her to get the video done for her art class. We should have gone away, had a break together, done something. But at the time, we couldn't. Malcolm didn't want to go on holiday, or even do usual stuff like tennis or biking. We thought he was being Mr Grumpy. It was only later that he revealed that a sudden swelling had come up in his groin, and he had had to have tests, and was deeply worried that it was a cancerous growth. (He'd had a scare a couple of years previously.) He couldn't undertake any exercise but wanted to keep his concerns private. It's in his nature to keep his worries to himself, not wanting to cause upset to anyone. I wish we'd known.

This was just one of a confluence of ill omens leading up to Vic's death: extra work at the office kept me back late; Vic's friends were all away; I fell sick with bronchitis; our new neighbours let their cat attack ours; there was study pressure from Vic's school. There was also the mysterious loss of Malaysian Airlines Flight MH370. How, in this electronic Big Brother age, could a plane of people just completely disappear? It unnerved and distracted me at a deep level.

All these factors on their own were manageable, but when they came in an onslaught they disturbed the equilibrium of the household, shutting out the light.

April 14, 2014, when Victoria died, was the day before a rare total lunar eclipse. Such an eclipse is known as a blood moon for the red hue the moon takes on when it falls under Earth's shadow. Vic had marked the event on her calendar. In a schedule, she had also marked the dates of full moons. The waxing and waning of the moon held significance for her in terms of the fragility of life, or maybe its inconsequence. She wrote in a poem: "She is the void between the glass and the frame, / A speck of dust on stained quartz crystal, / And the moon's veil between wax and wane."

Was she aware the blood moon has been used by prophets through the ages to signal doom? A biblical verse from Revelations says: "I watched as he opened the sixth seal. There was a great earthquake. The sun turned black like sackcloth made of goat hair. The whole moon turned blood red."

Perhaps Vic wanted to die before some sort of doomsday.

When she died she was wearing a necklace with a crescent-moon pendant. I haven't known she had such a necklace until Mohan, the security guard, turns up at our front door with it in his hand. A cleaner has found it amid some plants by the spot where Victoria landed. The silver chain is broken in two. The pendant has not fallen off; it's still clinging to one piece of the chain. I look at it closely. The crescent moon is coated with a brown-red substance—Victoria's blood.

Is this macabre memento, this blood moon burnished on silver and coated in my daughter's blood, a gift of the afterlife? I want to keep whatever I can of whatever is left of my daughter, even if just a drop of her blood on a metal moon.

17

FEAR OF HEIGHTS

One night, in the fraught months before Victoria's death, I had gone to Victoria's school for parent-teacher meetings. It was important to attend. This was Vic's final year of school and there were exams she was supposed to pass.

Malcolm had been delayed at a work meeting, so I was on my own. I got out of the taxi, running slightly late, and headed down the corridor to the senior library where the meetings were taking place. Other parents were bustling about self-importantly. A mother with whom I had been on nodding acquaintance terms for years said hello with a condescending smirk. Unlike Victoria, her daughter was one of the cool kids. The woman did occasional relief teaching at the school and I am sure she had a very different view of the school from mine.

Some of the teachers I wanted to see weren't there. Conversations with teachers who were there were depressing. The teachers were focused solely on Vic getting better grades. I realised with a wrench that we'd made a huge mistake sticking with this school, with its emphasis on academic success, but it seemed too late, too difficult, to pull Victoria out now.

Perhaps I was overreacting. The teachers were concerned about Victoria, but all assured me they thought she would "pull her socks up" and pass. They were teachers, authority figures. Surely they knew best?

I should have waited until Malcolm could join me, I thought ruefully. He would have stood up to the visual arts teacher who told me I must pressure Victoria to "deliver", to get her assignments done on time, to not be so "dreamy". You would never have thought Vic was studying a creative subject, where sometimes the magic happens because you dare to dream. Video and screen image-making were in Vic's DNA, the teacher declared, praising an "arty" video Vic made the year before, noting, "Besides, her father is a photographer."

Vic really loved drawing, I pointed out, but the teacher bluntly informed me Victoria did not draw well enough to succeed in Higher School Certificate. I said she did not like making videos and doing photography, but the teacher insisted: Victoria must stick with those subjects because she did them so well.

Vic's video project for HSC was called *Fear of Heights*. The teacher was worried she wouldn't finish it in time. "Your daughter procrastinates a lot," she said. Victoria did not "seem to have much initiative". I must ensure Victoria got her video project done over the coming school holidays, ready for the new term.

I felt I had been told off, was a bad mum. I allowed feelings of remorse and recrimination to overwhelm me, when I should have been wondering why on earth the teacher had not received information from the student welfare team that Victoria had some sort of attention deficit disorder. I had been told several years earlier that the information would be passed on to teachers at the start of every new school year. I'd blindly assumed this would be the case. I should also have queried with the arts teacher the wisdom of "Fear of Heights" as a topic for a student who was insecure and worried about exams. I should have said, "Let her draw. It doesn't matter if she gets a low mark. It's not all about the exams."

After the chats with the teachers, there was a presentation. A graduate of the school who'd gone on to university success spoke about the wonderful foundation of learning she'd got at the school. Vocational guidance officers spoke about the scores necessary to get into university, how to calculate them, what bands might be needed to get into various institutions, what countries they could offer information on, what courses were available. The post-school future they outlined was entirely about getting into a university. The parents around me seemed fine with this. Presumably they had bought into the notion that raising a child was primarily about getting him or her to pass exams that would enable them to be an economically productive unit of society. All the claims of being the best you could be, following your passion, learning to be inclusive, the notion that everyone had something to offer, were ultimately lies. It was simply all about being a banker, IT or human resources person, sales manager or accountant. Or a supportive spouse.

During the school holidays, Vic did get around to filming *Fear of Heights*. The camera is placed on the ledge of a stairwell of an apartment block. Vic appears on screen, holding a piece of tissue paper. A close-up shows words written in red: "Fear of heights". The camera draws back. Vic now has the tissue paper crumpled up, placed on an outstretched hand. She leans over the parapet and blows. The tissue rises and then falls away.

Two days later she would jump from the same spot.

ADJUSTMENT

I

18

SORRY, VIC

It is now three weeks since Vic's death. There is no preparing breakfast for her, ensuring she eats some of it, and has brushed her teeth and got dressed. No waiting at the front door to perform my goodbye ritual of tapping her backpack for luck and a "Bye, darling, love you," as she runs down the steps to the school bus. No more will my pleas ring out for her to stop and tie her shoelaces properly. I still get up at the same time. I am programmed to do so. And once Victoria is out the door, or rather I imagine she is out the door, I go and wait at the living-room window and pretend to watch the school bus pull up downstairs and enclose her. I hear the sigh of its pneumatic door, and a clank. And I remain at the window, as I always used to do, for that one last glimpse of Victoria, which was her seated, silhouetted profile as the bus swooped away down the hill. "Bye-bye darling," I whisper.

Other routines clamour too. Malcolm and I have had to return to work. There are bills to be paid. For

Malcolm, it's good to keep busy, to submerge himself in the demands of a daily newspaper. And he has a team around him of loyal picture-desk colleagues who will take care of him.

I take a few more days to return to the office. I've been wounded by past slights and am hopeless at reading office politics. I feel vulnerable. Cool-headed Jennifer from my social tennis group—one of those chiselled British women with a deep sense of duty and decency—drives me so I don't have to get a taxi or catch a bus.

As we pull up to the industrial facility that houses the newspaper's operations, I feel immense dread. My life is utterly changed, and yet returning to work means picking up the reins of continuity. It trivialises Victoria's death. How can resuming work and paying the bills be more important than mourning the loss of your child? Such grief will take a lifetime. Getting out of the car and going in through the entrance means suppressing that grief. It begins the farce of having people think you accept that she is dead. It is the beginning of "After".

Jennifer—who, before she married, used to take tour groups to a remote Indonesian island to see Komodo dragons—knows all about keeping calm and carrying on. She sits at the wheel, waiting. "We're here," she says breezily, apparently for a second time.

I get out of the car. And go in. "Sorry, Vic," I murmur.

Away from the security of home and in the uncompromising arena of the modern open-plan office,

I find that grief and shock have turned my brain to mush. I have the cognitive ability of a child. This first week, my hands shake over the keyboard. I stare at a sentence for hours. I plan to rewrite it or move a paragraph around, start to do it, and then forget what I intended. I cry at the most unexpected things and sometimes have to go home, unable to stem the tears. Fortunately, my bosses Lydia, Paul and Zakir understand and send me off with a sympathetic nod.

Emotions are triggered when I encounter something that doesn't belong in the tunnel-vision world of myself in a newspaper office. I go to the work canteen's Chinese stall to order fried rice and catch a glimpse inside the kitchen of a labourer washing the body of a dead piglet in a stainless-steel sink. The piglet's little head flops on the woman's arm as she wipes its skin, almost tenderly. I am transported to the funeral home, and to the sight of an inert body, stripped of most of its clothes, and holding a pale arm dangling off a gurney.

Gradually, though, a new routine of life tap-tap-taps a rhythm in time to my keyboard's soft clack of words, letters, punctuation. A kind of numbness sets in. It marks a total betrayal of Victoria and all the love a parent has for a child. It is unnatural. And yet there is no alternative, apart from death or the oblivion of antidepressants.

I take on extra duties, resuming work on a book, *50 Things to Love About Singapore*, although I have mixed feelings about the place now. I'd started the book before Vic died—another ill-advised move on my part. It took up too much time and made me bad-tempered as I scurried to edit slabs of prose while cooking dinner. "It's burnt again, Mum," Vic would say, as we smelt smouldering cheese sauce and rushed to grab the pot off the hob. "Just have to get takeaways," she would add, happily.

The book's editor asks me to lunch. Several Singapore colleagues are there. I listen politely to a long conversation about the virtues of French butter. We note that the butter on the table is not only French, but unsalted. A discussion ensues on how this affects the taste. The talk is superficial for a kind reason—they don't want to offend or upset me. I eat the food, swallowing it all. Someone sitting opposite me tells me she had a pet goose and it died in her arms and she has never been the same.

No one mentions my daughter.

In the security of our condo apartment, space opens for us to sit and think and remember. We have not changed anything in Vic's bedroom. The school bag, with its exercise books and tucked-away packet of chewing gum, sits on the chair by the homework desk, ready to be picked up and slung over a shoulder. The hairbrush is upturned on the dressing table. Posters for Avril Lavigne and Angus & Julia Stone adhere to the walls. I have, as a concession, turned off the heated hair straightener and put the school uniform back in the wardrobe. Apart from this the room is the same as it was the morning Victoria must have jumped out of bed, run past Mittens and Angelina, who would have been sleeping on the sofa, slipped out the front door and gone over the hill, past the tennis court and the remnant of jungle to the apartment block from which she fell to earth.

A narrative forms. Is it accurate? I don't know. But I need a narrative. It replays in my head, day after day: It was the first day of a new school term. I had got up at 6.45 a.m. to prepare toast and coffee for Vic. I tapped on her door to wake her. After a while, when there was no response, I went in and saw the empty bed, the covers hastily, untidily, thrown aside. She was normally so neat. It was her goodbye.

The bedroom. As the weeks have gone by I have been looking at what Victoria left behind, searching for clues. And, of course, any trace to prove and re-prove her existence. That she did, in fact, live, and was not some figment of my imagination.

I find a lot of clues under the bed and hidden at the bottom of boxes of discarded childhood toys. Diaries. Over the years I'd sometimes seen Victoria writing on pages within their pretty covers. I'd assumed it was a phase that she, like many girls, go through. I hadn't read them, too busy just trying to juggle work and home. Also, in a discussion once, some mums in a writing group had told me it was important to respect your daughter's privacy. One had read her daughter's diary and afterwards there had been terrible scenes and tears.

The message was that, as modern women, we owed our daughters the respect of having a place of privacy, where they could vent and express themselves.

If only I had questioned this. If only I had read up on the pressures young teens face these days, realised how vulnerable they are to outside influences, how they need respectful monitoring to see where their thoughts are leading, and who is influencing them, to be able to step in and shed light on any darkness.

Now, I force myself to look at these harrowing diaries of my late daughter and comprehend that they are an articulate testimony to a reality she could not express to us, for whatever reason. Pride? Shame? Fear of somehow letting us down? Not burdening us? A desire to seem the perfect child? Did she not see who we really were—just Linda and Malcolm, who loved her to bits?

The handwriting changes as she grows older. The writing goes from fat curls and the touching simplicity of "I had sandwiches for lunch" to the very last handwritten entry, a screaming tight scrawl veering off into unintelligibility: "I want to be dead. I just want to be dead. Maybe the reason I haven't mentioned it is because I don't want to stop feeling like I have access to this option. I just want to be dead is that too much to ask???"

Then a scrawl of a short sentence that is indecipherable except for: "Please xxx ME aat _____ ."

I'm a mess for several days after that.

That was her sign-off, I suppose. An unread cry for help. We did not hear it. We did not see it. Until now, when it is too late.

Again, I find myself constructing a narrative to try and control the story, although it is impossible to do so. The handwritten diaries end around the time Vic turned sixteen. They go from innocent musings on *Harry Potter* to the emergence of a longing to die, starting from fourteen, when she felt she no longer fitted in at school. She started going to the top of tall buildings and wondering if she could jump off and end her agony of self-doubt and disconnection.

These silent chronicles of despair tear apart my perception of myself as an aware, sensitive mother. They are too devastating to absorb. I close the diaries, for now.

We have our own signoffs to deal with: the answering of numerous condolence cards and emails. This is inconsequential in comparison with Victoria's scrawled plea of despair, but the cards and emails must be dealt with. Once we were three. There is something fundamentally wrong about signing off a letter or email without including Vic's name.

The first letter I write is to Vic's childhood friend Sivi, who now lives in Adelaide with her parents. I sign it "Love from Linda and Malcolm, and Victoria. XXXXXX."

However, this does not look right. It does not acknowledge that our family is ruptured, that Victoria has died, that we are in deep mourning for her.

I join a closed Facebook group for grieving parents, who offer advice on these mundane matters of existence, post-death. I learn to sign off with "Angel hugs from Vic." It is sort of cheesy but people I write to seem to be able to handle that. Some think it shows we accept that she is dead. Others like the idea of Victoria as an angel. I am not happy with either of those reasons. I know one thing, though: to not put Vic's name down, to not still make her mark in the world for her, would be inhuman. Imagine signing cards "From Linda and Malcolm". It erases Victoria's existence. It implies we want no mention of her.

What would Vic have wanted? "Oh Mum, live with it. Though angel hugs is okay. Grandma Sheila might like it."

Vic's other grandmother, my mother Elaine, isn't so happy about us continuing to acknowledge Victoria's existence, even as a memory. When we send cards that include one from Victoria, complete with the "angel hugs" sign-off, Mum emails: "Received your gift today of chocs, beautifully packaged, and the nice cards. You don't need to be taking Victoria's place with sending a card from her as we accept/know she has gone to a better place as was her wish."

———

No parents from school reach out to us. No students contact us. We later learn the school told parents and students that we did not wish any contact. We never made such a request.

19

SNOW WHITE

Without Victoria, life becomes lived in a kind of suspension, as if Victoria still *might* be here but has just gone away for a while. She is not physically here, but she is in my thoughts, night and day. Yet, every time I try and picture her face, or what she looked like, and how she moved in the world, and all the little characteristics of a human being, I can't see her at all. The visuals won't come. I can't even remember what my own daughter looked like. In desperation, I put up photos of her on a noticeboard above my desk and speak to them, as if that will bring her back. The images remain two-dimensional. They fail to evoke the living girl that was.

I can only clearly see her dead. Her long dark-brown hair lies against the white satin lining of the coffin. The coffin is white, too. I watch as a funeral home director tells me that parents like how it symbolises innocence. (Dark wood is for those whose time has come.) Victoria does not look innocent as she sleeps. She just looks shrunken and weary. Her eyes are shut, as if she wants us all to go away and leave her in peace. I see myself lingering, unable to leave. I put one last touch of rose blush on her lips. I look down on myself from above as I kiss her pale cheek. Mourners pull me back. "They have to take her now" are words that float, disembodied.

I hope that I will at least see her clearly alive in my dreams. But, if so, I go for weeks without remembering any. This is not uncommon among grieving parents, I learn, when I attend a child bereavement support group. Some go for months, years. I think I do dream, though, because when I wake up my eyes are crusted with tears and my cheeks are wet. Perhaps this lack of memory of her, even in a dream, is my mind protecting me during the early weeks of grief. I may not be emotionally ready to recall her presence to that degree. Would the fully imagined sight of her, standing tall in front of me, with her hair and eyes and youth, and her arms stretching in greeting, and the tinkling bangles she always wore, send me mad?

I would not mind going mad. It would absolve me of any need to go on coping, which is a kind of living hell. The simplicity of letting go, of shuffling about in a Valium-induced haze, is alluring. I lack the sort of ruthless ability that Victoria had to bring about a complete physical destruction of the entire human package. It is my fate to keep waking and find myself alive.

While I can't "see" Victoria, the sound of her voice comes back to me within weeks of her death. It comes only when I am not expecting it. It won't be invoked. So I resist the longing to call out her name. And occasionally, I am blessed.

Just weeks after Vic died, I am lying on her bed in her room, trying to feel her presence even if I cannot recall her. Her voice, or my inner voice, or a voice that is my inner voice that I project to be Vic, says, *Look in the bottom drawer, Mum. The bottom page.*

I go to the drawer that I have searched through several times. I know everything it contains: school exercise books and notes. But I find myself pulling out the last piece of paper at the bottom of the pile. I've never seen it before. It's a photocopy of a page from a child's fairy-tale book of *Snow White*. Snow White lies with her eyes shut, her dark hair tumbling on to the white satin lining of a white coffin, as the seven dwarves stare with incredible sadness. She is a beautiful young woman who looks at peace, far removed from the grief of the people she has left behind.

Hearing—or imagining that I hear—that gentle voice of Vic's and finding the Snow White picture are disturbing. Victoria, with her dyed brown hair and pale face in her white coffin, looked very much like the Snow White in the picture. She had the same serene expression, too. Not quite dead, as if a kiss might awaken her. Malcolm and I, and Fiona, Sharyn and Paula, slumped and devastated, gathered around the coffin like the dwarves. We shared the same expressions of shock, grief and despair as those wizened, wise creatures.

Victoria had wanted us to take a meaning from the picture, I know that much. Is this how she had envisioned events once she'd died—as some sort of fairy tale? It is a very child-like image. It does not grasp the sorrow of the bereaved. It does not begin to understand the depth of her loss for us. Yet by seventeen she had a quite sophisticated understanding of people and the cycle of life, too much so.

Or perhaps it is a reference to one of the poets she was reading for her English studies, to one of the dark versions of the fairy tale, to Anne Sexton's take on *Snow White*: "No matter what life you lead / the virgin is a lovely number: / cheeks as fragile as cigarette paper / arms and legs made of Limoges, / lips like Vin Du Rhône." Sexton's poem both romanticizes and mocks Snow White's physical appearance. Perhaps Victoria, in her beauty and virginity, is giving a last thumbs-down to society's values?

In contrast, even though the stepmother has lost her looks, she is much smarter than the "dumb bunny" Snow White. Yet in the end, after seeming to die, Snow White comes alive again.

20

APPOINTMENT SLIPS

It's too early. We need more time to grieve. We are still in deep shock and can handle only kindness from people. But exactly one month after Vic died, Malcolm and I have gone ahead and arranged an appointment with the school's student welfare officer, or counsellor as she is also called. Let's call her Mrs C. Amid our grief, questions are surfacing about the nature of Victoria's death. We have been alarmed to find in her pencil case and bag yellow Post-it slips that seem to be reminders of appointment sessions with the counsellor during the previous term. This is a shock as we knew nothing about such sessions. Mrs C did not mention them when she came to our home with her student welfare boss after Vic died.

We hope to find out what happened, what the sessions involved. What issues did Vic raise that might have led to her wanting to die? Was there anything to do with our parenting that she was upset about? We also hope to be consoled, and to learn more about our daughter and what she was like at school.

APPOINTMENT SLIPS

We have been told to report to the reception desk and someone will come and meet us. This is a new formality. Before, as parents, if we came to the school we would just stroll in. I had hoped to do so again, to see if I could feel Vic's presence in the corridor, to glimpse once more this world that we knew so little of, and perhaps to meet some of Vic's friends and fellow students and get an inkling of what should have been if life had continued as normal. Instead, we are met and bustled along the corridor—lined with class photos, oversized headshots of beaming prefects, and framed artwork—that we had walked along in our role as parents of a pupil for nearly ten years. Now we are visitors. I am bewildered by this change in status. It is one more disturbance in our new life of endless readjustment.

We are ushered up to the school guidance office. I have never been here before. I see the familiar figure of the guidance officer, Mrs E. She is something of a fixture in the school, but today her normally friendly face is downcast and closed. Mrs D, the head of the student welfare department, is also here. She has known Victoria from when she was a little pre-schooler and her husband taught her art.

They gesture for us to sit around a small table. The atmosphere is odd. It is bereft of something. I realise I am not getting any sense of sadness from Mrs D about Victoria's death. She is wearing a power suit with shoulder pads in the jacket. She is all business. Having to sit around a table adds to the unusual formality. It's like a meeting. It *is* a meeting.

Mrs D and Mrs E don't even attempt small talk. They are waiting. In bursts the counsellor. I recognise her from her visit to us after Vic died, when I had expected warmth, a hug, tears and an "I'm so sorry".

Mrs C plonks a briefcase on the table and, before even sitting down, declares, "I know you are looking at someone to blame and it isn't going to be me."

I gasp. Blame? It's a word that hasn't even crossed my mind. Why would I want to look for someone to blame, when, if we are going to use that word, it is me I would want to interrogate, curse and rail against?

She sits down. Silence. Malcolm and I look at each other. Mrs C doesn't look at us. Instead she rifles through her briefcase. Mrs D has her phone on the table. She seems to be constantly sending messages during our "chat". It dawns on me that she might be reporting back to someone about our responses.

It hits us that we are in the presence of corporate functionaries. Mrs C seems fearful and defensive. Her answers seem rehearsed. I hope in my heart that she is a caring person, but her responses are devoid of empathy. She seems to be thinking only about her employer and her obligations to the company. Our poor dear daughter had put her worries, her mental health, her life in the hands of people who could not help her.

I ask Mrs C how many times Victoria saw her for

counselling the previous term. She is vague. I have to ask repeatedly. Eventually she implies it was once. She adds that she maybe saw her four times altogether, including the year before. Malcolm and I have Post-it appointment slips indicating that Victoria saw this counsellor at least three times in the past term alone.

I ask what happened in these counselling sessions. Again, Mrs C is vague. Nervously glancing at Mrs D, she says something about breathing techniques and anxiety, but that Victoria being in the ensemble group of the school choir seemed to have settled her.

She then launches into what seems a sales spiel. "I am proud to be an employee of education provider [X], one of the biggest education providers in the world." She actually says this. She goes on about how the multinational organisation that owns the school follows the "most thorough" protocols for the welfare of its clients—(clients!)—how it has rules laid down, and a reputation.

Malcolm tries a different tack. He points out that students who were not academic high-fliers were made to feel second-rate. Mrs E agrees and starts to talk about what more the school could do for these students, but she stops in mid-flow. Mrs D takes over and steers the conversation away. Malcolm tells me later he saw Mrs D kick Mrs E's leg, presumably to indicate to her to shut up.

We change tack again and say we don't think the school did enough for Victoria, and for the grieving students in the aftermath of her death. We also note that one of her friends could have helped save her, that Vic had texted her on the Saturday night when that she tried to jump but couldn't do it.

I ask what the current protocol is and Mrs C says, almost defiantly and proudly, that students are to tell their teacher. I point out that this is useless as it was the weekend and Vic was dead by Monday morning. I suggest they create a new protocol, named after our daughter, in which students are instructed to tell any authority figure who is immediately available, be they a parent, teacher or police officer, or a trusted fellow student who is able to take action and notify an authority. This receives a lukewarm response.

The three women just want us out of the room and their lives, so they can retain their jobs and maintain the illusion of the school as one happy bunch of high-achievers and Vic's death as merely an unfortunate blip. I recognise that this is a disparaging and judgemental thing to say. I am sure they are loving mothers to their own children and care about those at school under their care. Yet who can blame me for feeling this way, especially when I learn later from outside sources that some at the school are saying they just want things "normalised"?

My life will never be "normalised".

Malcolm and I leave. In the corridors I notice Year Twelve students of Victoria's age rushing by in their striped uniforms, laughing, full of energy. I allow myself for a moment to hate them all for being alive.

We don't walk back to the entrance but depart furtively through the bus bay. I look back at the school, with its plaster façade, and realise how naïve I am, how innocent of the ways the place really runs, of the power rooms of the principal's office and the boardroom of the multinational owner. I believe the school let us down and we can't even hold them to account—not to apportion blame but to prevent this tragedy happening again to another poor student or her distraught parents. We haven't received any acknowledgement that we entrusted the school with our precious human being. That the school failed her. But I suppose such an acknowledgement might raise legal issues, issues they would want to avoid at all costs.

21

BYE MUM

It is a couple of hours since the meeting with the student welfare team, where the counsellor has been so evasive about her sessions with Victoria. Perhaps this tips me into madness. Or perhaps some residue of Victoria's extended consciousness, or an imagined part of it, is able to reach out to me in my despair. Later that day, back home in the apartment, I hear Victoria's voice tell me to *go to the ledge, Mum.*

I am lying on her bed thinking of her when the voice comes. It is instructive, not urgent, and I know instinctively she doesn't mean the small lift-lobby area where she jumped from, but the adjacent emergency stairwell, and one floor down.

I feel utterly confident I will find something there to help me keep going. I know Victoria would do that if she could. I cut some stems of bougainvillea from our pot plants to place at the spot where she died, as a gesture of reverence and of thanks for her message. I walk over the hill with its jungle area, tennis court and palm trees to the other side of the condo compound, to The Block. I put the flowers on the tiles where Vic's broken body lay. They're her favourite colours, purple and white. A passer-by will probably pick them up later and dump them in the shrubbery but never mind. It is important for me that the flowers are left there now.

I look up to check the note I stuck on the nearby wall last week, asking if anyone knew how Victoria died and letting them know how to contact me. The note has been ripped down. Bits of sticky tape remain stuck to the wall.

I take the lift to the tenth floor and stand at the little railed area from where she jumped, or flung herself, or slipped gently and let go. I look down and can see the blooms smiling up at me from below.

I turn from the ledge, even though it seems to be trying to lure me to follow Victoria down—*Just like that—jump!*—and go through a heavy door to the stairwell. I'm the only one up here on this early evening. I go down a flight of steps to a small landing area. This is the spot that Victoria means. It has a wide ledge of concrete, topped by cream-coloured stucco plaster that has been painted over in the same colour as the rest of the building. A person could sit quite comfortably on this wide ledge, dangle their legs out and feel above it all. More importantly, they would be completely undetected. A person could sit here for hours, looking out over the hill, over the blue-green tropical canopy. A person could listen to the birds, hear a kingfisher chatter, or a sea eagle high in the sky call to coax a young bird from a nest.

Standing there I don't see any message, but I believe there is one here. I kneel at the ledge to be right up close to it and begin a methodical examination. I mentally divide the ledge in squares to check off, from left to right, as if I am a pilot on a search-and-rescue mission. Fortunately, the sky is overcast; the soft light makes marks stand out more clearly than they would in bright sunlight.

And then I find them. The messages.

Victoria has cut very thin long lines into the paint. From a distance they seem to be just haphazard scrapes, but up close I can see they have been scratched deliberately. I don't know what with—the edge of a teaspoon perhaps, or a cutlery knife? Scissors? The lines are striated and look a bit like rolling hills. They are crisscrossed, suggesting agitation. Or the crosshatches of someone used to cutting such marks into their skin.

I look closer, past the marks. And find—a heart. I've seen the same heart drawn over and over in the margins of Vic's school exercise books.. Underneath the heart are words roughly etched in cursive script: "Bye Mum." The last "m" of "Mum" is incomplete and breaks off halfway with an abrupt wrench. Of course, it may not be Mum, I may be deluding myself, but that is what the scratchings look like. I gasp. Even at that dark time, Vic remembered me. She wanted, and wants, me to know that she loves me.

―――

The author Joan Didion has written about receiving messages from dead loved ones, despite her strong belief that this is not logically possible. After the sudden death of her screenwriter husband, she struggled to finish a newspaper commentary as he was no longer there to read it and help her polish it. She finally managed to complete it by imagining a message from him saying, *You're a professional. Finish the piece.*

She noted, "We allow ourselves to imagine only such messages as we need to survive."

However, the message I see on the ledge is not imagined. It is, literally, concrete. It was definitely carved by Vic, with the distinctive heart shape only she would have made. And I would not normally have gone back to that scene of tragedy unless I had felt Vic's urging at some deep level, and looked so keenly and closely at the paint on the ledge, fully expecting there would be a message there.

One has to be cynical: there was no logical reason for me to have been so convinced there was a message for me there, exactly a month after Victoria died. Was I simply allowing myself to hear Vic's "imagined" voice? Whatever the case, the message stops me following Vic over the edge to end the aching pain of loss. I keep going.

As the weeks and months pass, no teachers send us emails asking how we are doing. I email them directly, but each time the response comes back from the school head. I meet the head to see what progress, if any, has been made on our suggestions: the protocol on whom students should contact if someone tells them they are suicidal; and a proposal that vocational guidance officers include information on alternative futures as well as university study. The head does not seem very interested in these measures. I ask to see the counsellor's case notes on Victoria and he refuses. He does inform us, however, that the school board has commissioned an external audit into student welfare at the school. He stresses that this is in no way connected to our daughter's death.

A week or so passes. I speak to a lawyer who says we are perfectly entitled to see the counsellor's case notes about our daughter.

I am reading the school's newsletter online when I come across this:

CHANGES TO COUNSELLING DEPARTMENT
As part of our on-going commitment to student welfare we have recently reviewed the counselling structure across the entire school with a view to providing the most consistent and responsive service possible. The review took into consideration the needs of students, staff and the overall school community. In the Secondary School, [XX] will work full time with Grades 6–10, alongside Mrs C who will continue to work with Year 11 and 12 students.

I wonder to myself if this is the outcome of the board's "external" audit. It seems Mrs C is keeping her job but is now under supervision, or at least must work with another counsellor. She has signed the newsletter post, describing herself "Student Well-being Manager".

The school does not inform me of the changes.

22

SIGNS

About six weeks after Vic's death, to try and distract myself I go on a bus tour of quaint Singapore sites organised by ANZA, the Australian and New Zealand Association. I think it will be harmless, travelling around on a bus, lulled by its rhythm, anonymous in a chattering group of strangers.

Everything is fine until we pull up at a place famous for its singing caged birds. I see rows and rows and rows of cages on high poles in a field by a carpark, each with a songbird inside, and am transported to a vision of Victoria aged nine, when she attended a holiday camp that featured stories from around the world. In one programme she played a witch, or djinn, from a Moroccan tale called "The Pomegranate Tree". The story was based in the desert and featured the Berber people. A swirling, dervish-like djinn stole children, turned them into birds and put them into cages. The hero, a child, found the home of the djinn, tricked her and freed the children.

Vic hadn't minded playing the baddie. She had

thrown herself into the role of the djinn completely, relishing the chance to not be a Good Girl. She wrote in her diary of how the role empowered her. She had loved the opportunity to don a headscarf and costume, relished the textural feel of the robes and, above all, the djinn's sky-blue amulets. Traditionally, such amulets are worn as protection against the Evil Eye. Why would the djinn wear them? Who or what was she protecting herself from?

This had happened before middle school, and the sort of peer-group pressure that would make girls mock Vic for wearing a witch costume at Halloween. It was also before her retreat inwards, to the dangerous theatres of her rich imagination.

At the park I recall the children in the story who were turned into birds in cages. I feel souls calling to me for release. I don't know why but I also see rows of victims of Vlad the Impaler dying a horrible death. Vlad the Impaler is said to be the original Dracula, spawner of numerous teenage vampire movies. I burst into tears and leave.

Sometimes, in our attempts to make sense of tragedy, there are discoveries, both profound and sometimes ridiculous. Some of these can be explained away simply as humankind's instinctive need to see patterns, but I keep an open mind. Shortly after Victoria's death, I am flicking through Facebook photos of her friends. There is one photo of Vic, aged about sixteen, sitting with a school friend. It's probably some international day at the school. Vic is wearing black and white leggings with a vaguely ethnic pattern. Her friend is wearing a bright green leprechaun's hat, quite large and nicely made, and a distinctive black belt and buckle. The two of them are laughing and look happy.

The day after coming across the photo I go for a walk around the hill and gardens near our apartment and there, in the fork of a tree at the condo carpark, is a leprechaun's hat—very similar to the one in the photo. In this Asian country it is strange to stumble on a leprechaun's hat from Irish fairy folklore in a tembusu tree. I try to get it down but can't. The next day, it is gone.

Another time, on a Monday—the day of the week, now forever tainted—I go for a walk around the hill and end up sitting on the concrete steps above the tennis court. I stare at the sunset, not being uplifted by the spectacular red sky but plunged into despair that Victoria is not here to share it with me. A life of longing stretches ahead. I weep, quietly. Footsteps clatter behind me. A young man wearing walking boots and carrying a small backpack walks past, then stops and turns. "Are you all right?" he asks. I mutter something about feeling sad, missing someone. He pauses thoughtfully, then says, "I lived here many years ago in Singapore and I have had a week and a half, revisiting places. I love this hill and I came here to sit and watch the sunset."

He puts out a hand and adds, "My name is Johannes but you may call me John." He asks me again, "Are you all right?" I explain how my daughter Victoria died on the other side of the hill, that she had been unhappy. Then I add something about young people, how hard it is for them these days.

He looks up at me. His whole being seems full of joy—it radiates from his smile and even from his blond curly hair. He says, "No, it is not hard. There is so much to do, it is a wonderful life."

I say something about Vic seeing the glass half empty and he says that I mustn't be sad. "She is very happy now, so very happy. Here, let me give you a hug." We embrace, two strangers. Then he turns, walks off down the hill and is gone. The sun has not yet set. Everything feels unreal. I sometimes wonder if the young man was an angel. Or a leprechaun.

Malcolm, who is the strong silent type, casually reveals a sighting of Victoria. He was at our favourite shopping centre, Holland Village, mooching around, and decided to head to a place where he used to go with Victoria, a shop that sold kitchenware. He and Victoria would spend ages there, choosing a new spatula—silicone, rubberised or metal?—or looking at new equipment such as a mincer, or a dough mixer, or a pepper grinder.

Victoria liked the companionship, and the slow decision-making. As she was proficient at baking brownies, and helping Malcolm with the prep for his cooking, or cooking fried eggs or pancakes for herself, she was interested in what kitchenware worked best. And Malcolm liked having her along as she had a perfect eye. She would always look for the best quality item, the most useful and aesthetically pleasing. They would rarely find a perfect item. A new skillet pan became a shared quest, and even on holidays they would be keeping an eye out for shops that sold them.

Malcolm was strolling along the footpath to the shop when he saw Victoria walking ahead of him. He tells me it felt totally real. He could see only her back, but he was certain it was her, not someone who simply happened to look like her from behind. And then she was gone.

He tells me this has happened to him before, always at places they had visited when she was alive. "The supermarket?" I ask. "A voice asking you to make sure you get a packet of cinnamon rolls?" He nods and clams up. He doesn't want to talk about it. Such things are too easily dismissed.

23

THE DISCOVERY

It is a hot Sunday afternoon in late October, nearly seven months after we lost Vic, and the police have summoned us to the local station. We go by car. We have one now, only a leased one but Vic would have loved it, the ease of travel. The police station is in an area of public housing estates, a short drive from where we live. Whenever Victoria travelled to the mall on the condo shuttle bus, she would have gone past it.

The inspector awaits. He has been handling the police inquiry into our daughter's death. In the early days I would yell at him on the phone, demanding more information. Then I got worn down. A few months ago, he had told us the inquiry was concluded and we'd signed documents to say we did not request a coroner's inquiry. He had come to our home. I think it was a Sunday afternoon, like today. He'd been dressed in casual shorts and a polo T-shirt, as if it were his day off. Now, he wears a formal uniform of shirt and long trousers. He has summoned us to pick up what he terms "items of interest". He tries to be neutral, official, unreadable. But I know he is weary of me, this angry white woman with endless questions. Malcolm, a fellow male even if Caucasian, he feels sorry for.

The entrance interior is dimly lit by artificial light. I can make out shadowed walls painted pink, perhaps part of a governmental paint job lot decades ago. It is the pink of toilet tiles, with the sort of dirty grouting that surrounds stained urinals. The people swirling in the shadows, the civilians, or more likely criminals, are stained, too. Teeth are yellowed. Faces are dark scowls of rage or fear or guilt.

The inspector does not smile. He ushers us into a side room, perhaps for privacy, but leaves the door open. I am still conscious of pink and edit my thoughts to note that it is not a pastel pink but a putrid pink. I remember that the walls of the hospital where Victoria was born, here in Singapore, were tiled. The tiles were green, a repellent green, the green of baby poop.

We sit. The inspector addresses his words to Malcolm. He reminds us, in a mechanical voice, that there won't be a coroner's inquiry. The investigation is over. "Hence, you are able to pick up Victoria's personal effects."

The voice turns quiet and mumbles. "From where she ... at the ledge, and from when the police went to your house, her bedroom, collecting items of interest. The items are here. Take them."

He reaches below the desk and pulls out a tattered cardboard box. "Your daughter's things," he says.

THE DISCOVERY

She is reduced to this. A box that used to hold copy paper. We are in shock. We stare at the box. Our hearts are pounding. Our fists are clenched. The pain comes in waves. It grabs us, then tears us apart, again and again.

"Oh, and these, these are her slippers," he says, using the Singaporean word for sandals. He reaches under the desk and hands us a clear plastic bag. Vic had left the sandals neatly at the ledge she jumped from, and laid her mobile phone beside them, the inspector informs us. The way he pronounces the word "neatly" sounds almost approving.

Malcolm chokes back a gasp at the sight of the plastic bag with her shoes and phone. I am overwhelmed by my desire to touch Victoria, in any way. I reach inside the cardboard box. There are papers and a large manila folder, quite bulky. I pull it out quickly and peek inside.

The inspector flicks me a glance. Is it a warning? Is it something I would be better not to see? Or is it the uniformed functionary's lament: why is this civilian so disrespectful?

I start to pull out a black T-shirt. 'We washed them," he says. "But you still might find ... stains."

We are in the carpark next to the police station. Malcolm is clutching the cardboard box close to his chest. I am holding Victoria's laptop. According to the inspector, the police had looked at its files and they contained nothing of interest. He seemed adamant about that, but it makes me suspicious. How can he be so sure? Victoria used to type night and day. I am very interested in what the laptop might contain.

We approach the old white Honda we have leased. "Do you want me to drive?" I ask. Malcolm nods, teeth gritted, trying to hold it together. He tells me later that we had to sign some papers to take the items. I refused to do so. In the end he sorted it out. I don't remember this.

A week passes. The items of interest—desperate interest to us—sit on our dining-room table. Eventually, we pluck up courage. We try to open the computer first. It is locked. Malcolm eventually gets an IT person to access it. Suddenly we hear Victoria's voice, in written form. There are random diary entries over two years, original essays, poems and short stories, lists of songs she liked, favourite books, a description of her likes and dislikes.

There are transcripts of long-into-the-night online chats with Mary. They weren't just friends, it turns out, but best friends. Victoria was infatuated with Mary. Without naming her directly, she wrote that her friendship with Mary had been the most magical experience in the world. But Mary had not loved her back.

This does not faze us: we had sensed her confusion about her sexual identity during the past year. We had wanted her to be happy. I'd thought she was happy. Now I realise we knew little about her friends.

The computer also contained a detailed journal she wrote in the four months before she died. It ended when the school holidays began, two weeks before her death. It amounted to an extended suicide note. Together with the handwritten notes under her bed that dated back three years, it revealed that our daughter had lived in a separate, private world: one of dark thoughts, attempts at self-harm and purging, despair over low exam results, and a tendency to idealise the lives of her peers, especially the pretty, popular ones.

Some entries showed a clinical understanding of suicide that made me believe that Victoria could have been saved, with the right intervention.

Undated entries and poetry, created between 2013 and 2014:

> What is so annoying about people's stereotypical views of suicide: that only crazy people do it. You DO NOT HAVE TO BE CRAZY TO WANT TO KILL YOURSELF. Mental disorders are 90% of the time accompanied with suicidal thoughts, but obviously mental disorders are largely stigmatised. I know that I wasn't crazy when I first tried to kill myself (when aged 14). I felt like if I was such an oversensitive idiot, I would have absolutely no hope of success after school. ...There's a point when every part of you believes that you are hopeless, and you feel that your very existence isn't necessary. It was like all hope had just evaporated, and I accepted that the only way was to die. I just wanted the shit in my head to stop.

I had to vent. I was watching a suicide documentary on YouTube just before. Yep, just another 'normal' Thursday afternoon.

I've decided that maybe I should stick it out. Maybe.

Why can't doctors just find the gene that predisposes people to mental disorders and get rid of it?

But then she seems to give up:

The doubt rises like fluid flooding your lungs, rising higher and higher, until you feel yourself begin to drown. You gasp for air, but your throat won't let you inhale. And you wait for the lack of oxygen to poison your frontal lobes with piercing pain that you can't handle. I am close to losing it for good.

These thoughts were preceded by this poem.

The Virus
Waves of anti-dopamine inhibitors contaminate
The depths of my neurotransmitters,
Twisting and morphing anatomy,
Gradual and silent,
Lianas coil around synapses,
Tightening between the clustered
tree roots of connections,
A foreign virus that claims its homely settlement,
And elicits unyielding melancholy,
Relentless and cold,

THE DISCOVERY

> That antibodies cannot fight,
> And happiness cannot heal.

We had no idea. She was so beautiful, a head-turner. I never imagined she could hate her very self. I had no idea that her opinion of herself hinged so much on what others, her peers, thought. That our parental love was not enough. That I should have bared my fangs like a lioness and swept her up in my arms from a ruthless Darwinian world that wants to destroy such beauty, such kindness. Instead, I just thought, "My lovely daughter. You are a much better person inside and out than I am. I've made something better, with you. Welcome to the world, Victoria. It's going to love you."

I had been in la-la land. I felt I had won a prize, like Mother of Most Beautiful Baby Girl, or Mother of Miss Congeniality, or Mother of Miss Teen 17. She was my reward for all my own years lacking self-esteem and confidence. I would pinch myself for my good luck and think: She is my sun, she's beautiful inside and out. Like I said, la-la-land.

And so these laptop journal entries are a bittersweet gift. They give us a better idea of why she was in such despair. But at first I am overwhelmed by immense sadness and a longing for her non-existent future. My daughter Victoria—I want to shout her name to the universe over and over and over and in capital letters—
VICTORIA VICTORIA VICTORIA VICTORIA

VICTORIA VICTORIA VICTORIA VICTORIA. VICTORIA SKYE PRINGLE MCLEOD. VICKYSKYE (her Facebook name). VICKY (what friends called her at school). VIC (what Malcolm and I called her).

There is such touching, heartfelt awareness of her destructive thought patterns. She unflinchingly analyses why she has the urge to self-harm, and why she is driven to take that to the ultimate destruction of her very self, ending it all by jumping.

Initially, reading her descriptions of the depths of her anguish is a new devastation for me, even as it sheds new light on the whys. But, wonderfully, it is also healing. In Victoria's acute self-examination, she helps Malcolm and me to find a way out of the cycle of self-blame.

True, Victoria was infuriatingly indifferent to the fact that those who love someone will miss them when they die. But she does declare that she loves us. This is precious. This provides absolution. There is no sense of hatred, or anger at us. She is exasperated that we don't see her suffering. She doesn't exonerate us, and rightly so. Her death is still a challenge to us as parents, the realisation that even amid our love and hard work and plans for the future we failed her. There is no denying that the violence of her self-willed death is a rejection of our life together and of the world we created and were part of. But there's no fuck-you fury there, more an intelligent despair and bravery. And the acknowledgement of her love for us does provide us with a key to turn all that blame we feel to even greater love for her.

24

COMING OUT

It is three days since the discovery of Vic's writing and journaling on her laptop. I'm overwhelmed by what she has written. The feelings of panic and shock I felt in the immediate aftermath of her death return. I need help.

I'm in a room painted a soothing white. It contains two beige sofas with soft rugs lying artfully across them. Woven cloth cushions add texture. The effect would be Scandi-homely if not for the box of tissues placed prominently on the Ikea coffee table. The tissues are an essential work aid. The room is used by my grief counsellor, Patricia, who works at a practice owned by a long-time friend of mine.

The clinic cat saunters in. She is a fluffy, blue-eyed fixture of the counselling practice. I stroke her fur, as Vic had once done. When Vic was fourteen we'd discussed what she might want to do in life. She'd suggested she might want to be a counsellor. My friend had agreed to show her around and chat about what being a counsellor involved.

The practice is set in an estate of black and white

buildings from the 1950s, which once housed British officers and their families. The barracks have been restored and leased out to families and small businesses. Best of all, the great swathes of greenery are as yet undeveloped. There are mature trees of all kinds, and civet cats still come at night to feed on fallen tropical fruit. Pythons lurk in drains, hoping for a careless civet.

When we got out of the taxi, Vic looked around at this unexpected slice of rustic living and declared she liked the place. We went up old concrete steps and entered the bottom floor of one of the charmingly restored buildings. I had expected a dark interior, but my friend had brightened it up with white paint and modern furniture. She showed Vic the rooms where sessions with patients were held. Vic walked around, taking in the books on shelves and the general air of calm. She then befriended the gentle clinic cat, who had followed her, meowing. The cat served a useful purpose as she made nervous patients, especially children, relax and feel at home. Vic certainly felt at home. My friend lives in an apartment above the practice and Vic thought this was a wonderful set-up. "Away from layers of bosses and huge buildings. Your own private practice. Mum, I think I could do this," she told me. What she really wanted, though, was not to be a counsellor, but to be counselled.

The first entry. Wednesday, January 14. Exactly three months before she died:

I've known that I will never have a dazzling life, what with the grades I get. But if I keep carrying on like this, I might actually end up snapping. I've snapped before—and that was just when I was fourteen and didn't realize that I still had all this time ahead of me to fix things. I mean, what's the point in living when you know you're setting yourself up for a life of misery? It's also weird. How today I was in S's pool swimming and singing at the same time. Sunbathing on the grass. Smiling. And then the next, I'm crying about all these things that seemed so important at the time.

I honestly don't know how I'm going to cope when I get back to school. I know it's ridiculous to kill yourself simply because you failed high school. But it's knowing that without a single doubt, that you will fail at life, that you will essentially spend every day wishing you had spoken up and asked for help, that just takes over and makes everything else seem so unimportant.

I want to start writing again. I always have, but now on a daily basis. It calms me down when my thoughts get out of control. But on the other hand, it can also fuel them. Words, I mean... I just wish I could talk wholeheartedly to Mary. I know now that she'll understand. I would love to be completely open and honest with her again the night before school starts... If we can just tear down those walls we build up every day to speak the truth. Jeez, I'm 17 for God's sake; I should be over this sort of thing. I should be all cured and happy and sorted, like a filing cabinet.

But I'm not.

And now I sit on the sofa Victoria sat on, in a counselling room she walked around, stroking the cat she stroked. Perhaps that's why I am here. It is not just analytical and empathetic counselling skills I seek as much as the feeling of Vic's presence, how she recognised a sanctuary here.

I feel a kind of peace settle over me as one of the counsellors, Patricia—whom I have never met before—strides into the room with a scarf flowing behind her. She sits down and gives me a warm but frank stare that defies evasion. She has an inherent air of earned wisdom and trustworthiness.

In a soft Irish accent, she asks, "And how are you?" The way she says this is an acknowledgement that it's the opener to a ritualistic dance of counsellor and counselled.

I sip from a glass of water, shrug my shoulders and say, "Confused."

I have sent Patricia the laptop journals and she consults notes she has made about them. I hope for many things: some clue to why Vic did what she did; some insight into her state of mind; to take away something uplifting from the writing that will help me keep going.

A feeling almost of joy comes over me as Patricia praises the writing as "fabulous and articulate". That lost creature, the proud mother, surfaces. Patricia describes Vic's journals as the "most sane person writing about mental problems". She gives me some insight when she says, "However, with Vic's lack of problem-solving skills, she was unable to work out a solution. Her death was an outcome of that ruthless sanity."

Ruthless sanity. I file that one away.

I say I am sad the transcripts and journals hardly mention Malcolm and me. Patricia explains that "she takes that love for granted ... Teens are often like this".

I ask her about the transcripts of online conversations between Victoria and Mary. The two friends would text each other for hours, talking about their insecurities. Mary would seek help for her need to self-harm by cutting. Patricia says Vic clearly understood what she was doing. "With Mary, she acts as a counsellor, giving advice that seems well-researched."

I am pleased Patricia has picked up on that. In Vic's journal she has a lot of asides about her own psychological state, such as:

> I would like deeply to eat my feelings. It's what you might call a non-cataclysmically-but-still-destructive-coping-mechanism. I'm neither hungry nor full. I'm neither bored nor active. God knows I should be running around using up adenosine tri-phosphate stores and diligently studying like an actively functioning young adult.

In her texts, Victoria advised Mary what to do when she was panicking and wanting to self-harm:

Vicky: I'm here, keep holding on until it passes. I promise you, it goes away.
Mary: I can't do this.
Vicky: Yes, you CAN.
Mary: I can't study.
Vicky: You're a whole lot stronger than you think you are.

Further on:

Vicky: Do you feel okay? Go get an ice cube. That's a much better distractor than the alternative. You come straight back to me.
Mary: I want to care about myself. I want to know that it's not the right thing but I don't.
Vicky: What I did is I put my blades in a drawer folded up in a note I wrote to myself, reminding me that I am worth more than that. And sweetheart, having at least one person is much more than a lot of other people have.
Mary: I was going to go and cut my arm open, but accidentally, not to die, but just to calm down.
Vicky: Don't ever plan that again, god don't.

One thing I don't raise with Patricia is what Vic meant when she wrote the night before they went back to school to start the new term that she would love to be "completely open and honest" with Mary. Did she blurt out something to Mary, tell her she had feelings for her? And if so, how did Mary respond?

Or did she hold off doing this until that last weekend—before the start of a dreaded new school term?

I'll never know the answer as I didn't get the opportunity to ask Mary or her mother about this, and we have not been able to access Vic's phone to see what messages she sent and received that final night because we don't know her password. The Samsung Android people have told us we will lose all the phone's data if we can't get into it. We keep the phone charged in the hope that some day someone might be able to help us solve these mysteries.

Even before getting the laptop back, Malcolm and I had known that Victoria was uncertain about her sexual orientation. We had found references to it in the handwritten diaries that were under her bed and hidden at the bottom of cardboard boxes of discarded childhood toys. The diaries went back several years. When she had just turned fourteen she was copying the other girls in her class and gushing about boys. She wrote about an American TV show called *The Suite Life on Deck*: "I love drooling over one of the main characters, Cody (Cole Sprouse). I can't see how other girls don't think of him as the hottest and cutest guy on the planet. Okay, he plays a nerd, but a super good-looking one. And his character is sensitive and totally adorable. If he really is like that in real life, I would keep a poster of him, and kiss it every night."

She had gone on to hint at what was to prove her downfall in relationships, and maybe her whole life—the urgent and absolute need to find a soulmate: "Next year, I think I'd feel ready to have a proper boyfriend, one who really likes me for me. You see, I dream of my first boyfriend being my soulmate and future husband. Of course, the chances of that happening are pretty slim, but nonetheless, I'd put it on my Christmas Wish list and rely on fate. Right now, I'm just crushing on boys from afar. I don't feel ready for that kind of commitment. And right now, I just don't feel... ready."

By the time she was nearly seventeen and had gone through two unrequited infatuations with girls at her school, she was writing: "OK, I'm confused. One minute I like girls, the next, I like guys. I had decided that I would be an active member of the online LGBT community. I still want to. And I still want to be with a girl. But I would make an exception with one specific, unique guy—actor Tom Holland. I never really get very attracted to guys in movies. But Tom Holland actually makes me seriously consider wanting to be with him. Which takes me by surprise. Now I am confused whether I'm bi, or gay with the chance that I could make a special exception."

But next minute she was saying of a girl at school: "When she puts her arm around me, I can't help thinking for a second that maybe, just maybe, she likes me more than just a friend, that she feels something, too. But the second I think that, I have to remind myself that she doesn't. She just doesn't. I have to deal with it. And then, I wish she wouldn't put her arms around me."

She had dropped hints to us that she found girls attractive. We didn't mind what her sexual orientation was: to us she was still a kid searching for her identity. We wanted her to feel supported. When journalist friends invited us to a private book launch at an "alternative" night club, we took Vic along. We stayed only a short while and didn't drink but we wanted Vic to see LGBT people dancing and hugging each other to the beat of music in a way that was no big deal.

Vic did not say much. I realise now that, for a teenager, it was probably embarrassing to be in such a place with her parents. I feel cross with myself for not thinking things through. I wonder, now, if she was sad. Sad, because she could not articulate to us her real feelings in a forthright way.

In the taxi home Malcolm and I tried to make conversation with her—"That drag queen in the ballgown, wow"; "The lip synching, pretty cool"—but there was an undercurrent of detachment we were dimly aware of, even then. It felt as though Vic was removing herself from us and even from her friends. Most teenagers would be texting friends about going to a drag queen nightclub with Mum and Dad but this was not happening.

Being gay in Singapore means legal problems. A law making homosexual acts illegal is still on the statute books, although there is a tacit understanding that it won't be enforced. Vic noted in one of her diaries: "Oh even worse, I am gay in Singapore, where you can get jailed for being gay." It was unlikely she would ever be jailed, but it showed she was aware that being gay was frowned on—could even lead to rejection—by the society we lived in.

When we met with Mrs C at that awkward gathering after Vic died, we had told her our daughter was struggling with her sexual identity. Mrs C had replied incredulously, "What, Vic, gay? No way!" It was not the response we wanted from someone who had been guiding our child's future. We had expected empathy and lack of judgement, an open mind to the possibility of alternatives to the mainstream.

Vic tried to be her authentic self, whatever society thought. She drew endless love hearts in the margins of exercise books with the intertwined names of herself and whichever girl was the object of her attachment at the time. There was endless lovelorn poetry in those margins too. No teacher ever commented.

One of the early crushes, let's call her Anna, was the subject of a lot of daydreaming in the margins. The diaries showed that Anna didn't return the love, even though Vic became so desperate she tried to learn about anime, of which Anna was a big fan. Vic was aware this desire to please was not true to herself. She wrote: "I can't completely be myself with her. I want to be friends with someone I can be, and who can as well."

Although the school has told the parents not to contact us, one day I think to heck with this silence. I'm going to reach out.. I find Anna's mother's email address in the class contact list and ask to get together with her and her daughter. I choose a neutral venue, one of the many outlets of The Coffee Bean and Tea Leaf chain, and find a seat outside, where we can talk in private. I reason that if Anna feels uncomfortable she can easily leave. Suicide is a difficult topic. I cannot begin to imagine the confusion and heartbreak suffered by a student who has lost a friend this way.

The meeting with Anna will be the first of several at this café with Vic's friends or their mothers. As it turns out, I needn't have worried that the students and their mothers would be overcome and have to leave. Like the others, Anna is eager to talk about Victoria. Even when tears flow, she wants to help me honour Victoria and try to find meaning in her death. A talented musician, Anna sang with Vic in the school choir. One of the nice things she does is tell me the names of Vic's favourite singers, songs, performers and albums. It is a gift. Vic was always listening to the tunes on her phone but I had no idea what they were. The list includes teenage stuff like *The Perks of Being a Wallflower* soundtrack, Imagine Dragons and Coldplay. There are also songs from my generation, such as "Goodbye Yellow Brick Road".

Once Anna and I feel at ease I mention how I thought Vic might have had a crush on her. At a school concert, they had sung together side by side in a choral performance and Victoria had told me afterwards that Anna was special to her. At the time, the meaning of what Victoria was perhaps trying to convey was lost on me, but I had been thinking about it a lot since she died.

Anna seems surprised that Vic might have felt that way, so I wonder if I should have mentioned it. Then she pauses dramatically, turns to her mother and announces, "Actually, Mum, I am gay, and this is me coming out." They look at each other in total surprise, share a mother-daughter look—of what? Love? Connection?—and giggle. Then Anna's mother says, "Oh, okay" in a tone that implies they will talk about it later but she is cool with it. I feel that Vic is with us at the table, laughing, saying, "Yes, yes."

Three years later, when Vic's friends have left school and are scattered around the globe, I send out emails and messages, telling them I am writing a book and seeking nformation. I learn from Anna that she and Vic became friends when they were about thirteen and met in French class. She writes: "Vicky and I were not best friends, but we had a lot of fun together and I really loved having her around. We had a similar taste in music, and I loved to share songs with her, and talk about artsy things like that. We were also in choir and vocal ensemble together."

Victoria seems to have been able to come out of her shell around Anna, but she kept quiet in school group situations, as evidenced by this anecdote of Anna's: "I remember once during a swimming carnival in Grade 9, the races had to stop due to a thunderstorm, so the teachers just let us dance to pop songs while we waited for the storm to pass. I was so surprised when Vicky came down from the grandstand to join in, and I remember saying, 'Victoria?' incredulously. In reply, she just rolled her eyes and said, 'I'm not *that* shy.'"

In hindsight, Anna says of Victoria's belief that she might be gay: "I didn't know ... I'm so angry at myself, because there were so many obvious signs for so long, and the majority of our friendship group weren't straight. And even if we weren't open about our sexualities back then, we were certainly open about our support for them.

"I didn't know she had a crush on me at all. I actually can't think, even now, of any point in time where she dropped even the subtlest hints that she liked me. Knowing now that it had gone on for so long, I thought there would be something that I could have pointed to and said, 'Maybe that was a hint.' But honestly, I can't think of anything at all. If I had known she was struggling with her sexuality, there would have been so many things I would have approached differently, just to make sure she knew it wasn't something I would have been uncomfortable with at all."

I ask another of Vic's friends, the outgoing and kind-hearted Hannah, whether she knew Vic was gay. By now twenty-one and studying at university in Australia,

Hannah replies: "For some reason I feel like she'd told me. Thinking back on it, most likely two or three in the group of friends were gay though, or bisexual etc. So it wouldn't have been surprising. They often joked that I was the 'token straight person', completely breaking the stereotype of having a 'token gay person' you often see in movies. I don't think she was very open about it, but I feel like I knew."

Why, in the end, was it Mary she was infatuated with? Hannah doesn't know. "Mary was this little pint-sized girl ... She always seemed to have one person she clung to. When I arrived it was [X] but she left at the end of Year 10, so it must have gradually become Vicky."

I have to acknowledge that Mary gave Victoria love, attention and understanding. Vic left this message for her in her journal:

> (To be sent after graduation)
> Okay. I'm not really good at this saccharine lovey-dovey thing, but since I don't know exactly when I'll see you again, I think that it's appropriate to try. I'm also going to try using some fancy words. It could be five years (if either one of us has an existential crisis during/after university and needs to fly over to bring them back to reality). It could be ten years (before your wedding and you need someone to throw you a smashing bachelorette chimera/soiree). Or it could be fifty (if we grow old alone and become raging dog/cat ladies and need someone to drink tea or tequila with).

I'll start off by saying that hon: I honestly don't know what I'd have done without you. Thanks for being part of our coterie's Fan Girl Society (i.e. someone who shares my love of TLOTR and TFIOS). Thanks for being my Bio/Business buddy. Thanks for talking. Thanks for listening. Fuck it, thanks for breathing.

I'll never forget singing 'They're Taking the Hobbits to Isengard' at the top of our lungs while attempting to bake that Elf bread. I'll never forget (unsuccessfully) constructing a fort out of your bed sheets at four in the morning. I won't forget singing in the Honesty Gym (enhanced by its great 'acoustics') at midnight. I won't forget talking about all the things we were so afraid to talk about, in said gym in the middle of the night. I don't know about you, but I think those nights will always be some of the most emancipating times of my life.
Love,
Pringle/Chippy/Skye/The Cloud/ The One And Only Vicky.

I reach out to another of Victoria's friends, Sophie, who first met Victoria when she was fourteen, and became close to her the following year. Sophie writes: "In Year 10, Victoria messaged me saying that she thought she was first bi. However, in about Year 11 she came out to me as being gay and that she had planned on coming out to the other members in our friendship group."

Sophie also helps me gain more insight into Victoria with her comments on what their friendship meant: "She was so full of life. She would always be there for her friends and would always listen to others and provide the best support. She was the glue that held our friendship group together.

"Victoria, especially in Year 10, opened up to me and became more confident within herself around me. As well, she shared any insecurities she faced. Victoria also helped me through a multitude of issues I faced in Year 10, and I share such fond memories of our friendship. However, I wish that she were as confident and happy being herself as when we were the only ones together—when other people were with us she would not be as confident in herself. I remember she had told me that she found it very difficult to be as social and confident when there were many people in certain situations. I also wish that she could have seen how much of an amazing person and friend she has been to me and many others, as well as seen how intelligent she was."

One day, in those last months of Victoria's life, a package from Amazon had arrived at our flat addressed to her. Inside were a pair of military-style, lace-up brown leather boots. They were not at all elegant—Doc Martens and made for stomping. Vic put them on and looked fabulously hip, with her skinny jeans and long blonde hair. But for some reason I hit the roof. I said they were totally unsuitable for a country with a hot humid climate and where did she expect to wear them? And look at the price tag. *You saved up your allowance to spend on a pair of boots you can't even wear here.* The whole nagging mother deal—I'm sure many parents have been there.

I recall my tirade like it was yesterday. Why hadn't I just let things be? I suppose the boots shouted "dyke" and despite thinking I was cool with that, it seems I was not emotionally ready to go there. Now I wish I could hug Victoria and say how beautiful she looked in those boots.

Patricia tells me all parents have regrets like this. But I think of how wounded Vic would have felt, and there are no excuses, there is no consolation. I don't know where the boots are now but I have kept the red and yellow checked lumberjack shirt I found in Vic's wardrobe after her death. It is so unlike the floaty florals she usually wore. I make sure the moths or mould don't get to it. I take it off its hanger now and then, wrap a sleeve around my face, feel the coarse fibres against my cheek and tell Vic I'll take care of it forever.

25

DISCREPANCIES

The discovery of Victoria's journal on her laptop sheds light on what may have occurred during counselling sessions at the school. On March 9, 2014, she wrote:

> Well, Mrs C knows I self-harmed. I'd never have considered she'd work that out. Thank God she hasn't told them. I briefly recounted what happened on the 27th. Leaving out the whole death thing, of course. But I explained that it was like those thoughts of hopelessness had gotten out of control and I wanted escape. She thought I meant by the blade. I was talking about death.

There are several more references to her counselling sessions with Mrs C. However, there is no way of proving that what she wrote actually took place. This is important because, when we eventually get to see various counselling notes from the school, in none of them is there any indication of counsellors identifying Vic's self-harming. This is despite Victoria's reference to it in her journal entry just over a month before she died.

The school counselling notes cover over two years of in-house messages about Victoria, and sessions when she saw counsellors. Or perhaps it is just one counsellor; this is not clear. We are not offered notes of the time when Vic was ten and saw the counselling team of the time. I am so overwhelmed about receiving any information from the school that I initially fail to notice this.

Early notes from the start of the two-year period contain some vague emails. The counsellor has organised a meeting with teachers. Alarmingly, she writes that the subject matter regarding Victoria is too sensitive to commit to email. We were never told this.

After a meeting to discuss whatever was deemed too sensitive, there is an email to another student welfare person in which the counsellor declares: "I will still continue counselling Victoria." When I talked about this with outside counsellors at a private practice and shared some of the documents, they pointed out there were no case notes for fifteen months after that. If Mrs C continued to counsel Victoria, where are those case notes? Worse, why was no risk assessment done?

And why is there no mention in these two years of notes and emails of a psychological assessment that was carried out in March 2006, a copy of which we gave to the school and discussed with the then counsellor. According to the assessment, index scores had revealed a greater than average correspondence with attention deficit hyperactivity disorder (ADHD), of the inattentive rather than impulsive type. The report also noted atypical levels of perfectionism, together with some tendency towards anxious-shy behaviour and somatic symptomatology—a condition where a person feels extreme anxiety about physical symptoms such as pain or tiredness.

Confusingly for us as parents, the report had concluded that, while Vic "demonstrated the greatest difficulty on a test of numerical operations, there was little indication of a specific disability". The last part had made us naïvely think her problems were not serious.

The counsellor had assured us the important information about Vic's ADHD would be passed on to teachers every new school year. It seems this had not happened. We are alarmed to find out that vital pieces of information had not been passed on to new counsellors and teachers after the school was sold around 2012. The new owners had brought in their own people and made new appointments.

The external counsellors also point out there should have been a note in Vic's school files that in 2008, on the personal recommendation of the school counsellor, she had been treated by a psychologist for trichotillomania, compulsively tearing out of hair. The hair-tearing had happened when she was about eleven. She had been devastated when her first best friend at the school dumped her. (This girl was the weeping prefect at her funeral.) Vic had been so distraught she had begun pulling out not only her hair but her eyebrows and eyelashes. The Mayo Clinic in the United States describes trichotillomania as "a mental disorder that involves recurrent, irresistible urges to pull out hair from your scalp, eyebrows or other areas of your body, despite trying to stop". It occurs most often between the ages of ten and thirteen and is a way of dealing with negative or uncomfortable feelings, such as stress, anxiety, tension. The act of doing it can provide a sense of relief and feel satisfying. It is believed to be caused by a combination of genetic and environmental factors.

I now know that compulsive hair-tearing is a form of self-harm. At the time, while I was horrified and alarmed, I thought it was a phase Vic was going through. I had no idea of its terrible implications and what it might portend. After a few counselling sessions Vic seemed to recover. She stopped pulling her hair out. As a parent you just want things to get better, to keep moving forward. I had no inkling of the depth of her disturbance. She had always been a wonderful, funny, glorious child, but as the bereavement counsellor Patricia tells me, "You see what you want to see."

Malcolm and I consult a lawyer, who advises there is no legal precedent to sue the school over any possible lapse of duty of care. Even if there were, he says, it would not be worth pursuing through the courts because it would take a devastating emotional toll. This is not what we wish to hear, but we realise it is wise counsel.

We worry that Victoria's classmates may not be getting the advice and counselling they need in the wake of her death. But there is little we can do. We are exhausted and utterly saddened. I take heart from the words of Pope Francis, who in a list of advice for happiness, said: "Live and let live." We decide to focus on goodwill with the school and discuss setting up an annual prize in Victoria's name for original creative writing. The school says it is also amenable to putting up an artwork and a plaque.

We ask if teachers can share anecdotes or memories with us. We can't ask them directly as any emails we send to them get flipped straight to the new principal—the former one has left—his secretary or the vice-principal. Eventually a list of anecdotes arrives from the principal's office. We try to find comfort in them. One teacher writes, touchingly: "Sometimes teachers struggle to remember the quiet ones, but an English teacher never forgets the writers. And Victoria was a writer. In the corner of my classroom I have a writer's corner where I put little gems of student creativity. I tell students their words will stay long after they have gone—to inspire those to come. Victoria is there."

These words distract us for a while. But unpleasant facts won't go away. We have to face them. Vic's laptop journal has entries with a very different version of her counselling sessions from the school's account.

One month and one day before she died:

Stuff to tell Mrs C ... wanted to be by myself again, incessant suicidal ideation, just fix me. Please fix me or I can't be here.

After her visit to our house when Vic died and the distressing corporate-style meeting a month later, Mrs C never contacts us again, to our knowledge.

I find this untitled poem by Victoria in her computer:

Red eyes with tears, fossilised,
I am almost peaceful.
There is a strange acceptance about expiry,
Finality.
Closure.
Nothing more can taint your head.
No more voices can eat away
The gossamer strands of thought
Like silkworms devouring matter,
Piece by piece,
Until there is nothing left
But an empty gap.
The worms are hungry.
You provide no nourishment.
No seeds planted, waiting to grow
And bloom with motivation
That serves as a well.
It has been drained through

Your eyes. Perpetually saturated.
You're as helpless as a rotting leaf.
The wind comes.
You blow away.

Nearly a year after Victoria dies—the week the results come out of the HSC exams that Victoria would have sat had she lived—we learn of a new tragedy. A boy who was in Vic's home-room class has died suddenly. He had left the school at the end of the exam year with his Year 12 cohort and was technically no longer a student of the school, but the coincidence is shocking.

I look at the class photo, taken the previous February. Vic and the boy stand in the same line, with only one student separating them. Both stare out with youthful, expectant faces at the future ahead of them. Yet eleven months later both of them are dead.

Malcolm and I want to know more. We visit the new school principal, a short rotund man with a glad-handing grin. He is likeable and chatty, yet evasive. I feel this as soon as I walk into his office and it unsettles me. All I want is openness. Initially he tells us the boy died after fooling about on heavy machinery and falling. Eventually, after I muster up determination and ask him several times, he concedes there are several versions of how the boy died. That is all I can extract. We leave, defeated.

Many months later I meet up with the boy's mother. It isn't easy to reach out to her: I don't want to interrupt her in her grief and get swamped with fresh sadness. But I have a need to know that I can't ignore. I learn that, like Vic, the boy had attention issues. He was seeing the same counsellor although, unlike us, his parents were kept fully involved in the process. The boy was not a friend of Vic's but they knew each other at school for several years and had done art and drama together.

During a tearful afternoon, his mother generously shares memories of her boy, her love for him, and confirms that, like my daughter, he took his own life.

26

BULLIES

And what of Vic's exam results, the ones she dreaded receiving that first week back at school? In her journal she had written:

> I might not make it this year. I know that when I see those grades, I will either jump for joy, or jump off the top floor of this condo.

She received percentage passes in the 60s and 70s for three subjects, including English Advanced. This was despite her having panicked during the English exam. The English teacher, a kindly person who genuinely cared about Vic and recognised her talent as a writer, told me what had happened. At the halfway point of the exam, students were meant to hand in a certain section, but Vic had handed in all her papers by mistake and was too mortified to go up to the administrator and ask for them back. She sat through the last hour of the exam in agony, finally in the last few minutes putting some creative writing down on a spare bit of paper that the teacher later graded for the exam. It pains me now to think of Victoria sitting there, under that stress, unable to speak up and ask for help.

She had two near passes of 45 and 47 for Business Studies and History. When it came to the finals, with more study, she would probably have passed. Only Biology was not great, at 30 percent, but she could have dropped that for the finals.

Emailing her friend Anna three years later, I ask why she thinks Vic found school so awful. Anna replies that it can't be pinned down to one specific thing, but if it could it would be the unhealthy competition that the school—intentionally or not—fostered. Grades 11 and 12 were when it really started to present itself as a problem. "There were times when we would compare our grades, and if she came up even slightly short, she'd get embarrassed and frustrated," Anna says. "Ironically (and this was something I said to her several times), her grades were far from bad. It was the difference between her 80 percent and my 82 percent that would upset her. And I didn't even get higher grades than her all the time, especially in English."

Victoria wrote several pieces specifically about teachers at the school. In one of her school exercise books, English, I stumble on this, hidden under the headline "Soliloquy: Act 3, Scene 1, lines 64-98. Hamlet explores the philosophical nature of the world":

The tutor was one of those narrow-minded people who see the world like a newspaper. He commented when taking the register that he lived in a city called Wells. I nodded. There was also a song called "Wells" and I should look it up. I nodded. "I don't need this," I said in my head. But life always gives you what you feel you don't need. "I'll let you get back to your work then," he said dismissively. Some people laughed. I put on my smile mask. I stayed silent.

In a handwritten, soft-cover diary, possibly from when Vic was sixteen, there is this:

My Home-room teacher marked my presentation. She was apparently both impressed and shocked, because I don't say anything in Home room, but according to her, I present really well. I don't really see what all the fuss is about. All I did was speak loudly. Anyway, she told me to stop being shy.

It makes me so mad when people say that kind of stuff. I don't have an "off" switch for that. It's like, you can't tell an outgoing person to just stop being confident. And "shy" is such a stereotype. I'm socially anxious. That means I can't raise my hand in class discussions—and I hate those times when the whole class doesn't know the answer, but I do, and I'm desperate to say it, but something inside me won't let me. Believe me, if I could, I would.

Two years or so after Vic died, in a fit of fury and despair I send this to the teacher in question. He is shocked, but to be fair he does send me a photo of Vic I have never seen, of her at a school camp in Vietnam. I value the gesture.

Another time she wrote:

> We had Art today. I don't like Mr X. I'm going to have to put up with him for the rest of the year. He's about as instigating, let alone approachable, as a reformatory martinet disguised in a powder pink tie. He doesn't like me because I'm not a straight-A student and I don't participate. Which is yet again more bitter irony because I used to love art and it was my best subject. Apparently he wants to interrogate every one of us every few weeks to check on our Body of Work progress. I want to explore a disorder and I don't exactly want to give a Social Anxiety 101 lecture to him. It's a private kind of thing.

When I ask Vic's friend Sophie about the school, her answer makes me think of the crying prefect at the funeral, one of the "cool kids" who excluded my daughter. Sophie says, "The popular people in the year either made fun or would judge her or spread rumors of the group in general, because our friendship group was not very close to the main popular 'cliques'."

This revelation—that the students made fun of

Victoria—is news to me. It breaks my heart all over again. But at least I know more about what she went through. In her writing, Vic does not directly mention other students belittling her, but there is mostly a strong sense of her always being on the outside, not allowed in. I come across only one reference to bullying, in a handwritten diary:

> Thursday, September 8, 2012. Algebra
> I'm trying to type this while Mr H isn't looking. I don't get what the problems are on the board, but I'll go over them at home with my maths tutor ... Hey! I just realised that there are only eleven days left of term! I just want to get away from school. Realistically, my school isn't bad. No one takes drugs or alcohol, no one gets beaten up. It's worse to be bullied than to be an outsider. But it does make you lonely. Being an outsider, I mean. And being bullied, too.

Victoria never told us she was bullied. If she had been, most likely she would have felt ashamed she was in the situation, and I suspect she would also have wanted to protect us from it. She would have seen her problems, wrongly, as yet another "burden" for Mum and Dad to bear in their harried lives.

The comment in her journal is the only direct reference to being bullied, but three years later I learn more from Ellie Carson, a student in her home-room class who did the more highly regarded International

Baccalaureate, rather than the Higher School Certificate that Vic was undertaking.

Ellie willingly gives written consent for her full name to be used in this book. She tells me: " Unfortunately, there was a lot of bullying and I even told several teachers about it and who the problem people were. Vicky's group of friends were all really nice, but I know they were the target of a lot of nasty comments. The entire group collectively was then roped in together and I know that a lot of the kids doing HSC could be very nasty and exclusive.

Ellie and I have a Messenger conversation, which she has allowed me to quote from:

> *Me:* Tx, this helps a lot. I always wondered why no parents contacted us after Vic's death. The class mother was very offhand. Never even sent us flowers. I realise now they probably felt guilty.
> *Ellie:* Her son was one of the main people behind the attacks—I'm not surprised she had nothing to say.
> *Me:* I guess I just want an example of what they did... did they make fun of her not being able to speak up?
> *Ellie:* It was more that they used it to their advantage. They would make mean comments, and because she wouldn't they would get away with it. Mr [X] was the teacher supposed to help anyone in our year and he had personal favourites in the group... [but] if anything Vicky probably felt like it wasn't a big deal to everyone else because it was downplayed by the school.

Me: How were you affected by the bullying? What did they do to you?
Ellie: They did a similar thing to my group of friends—called us names. "Dream team" was one. I wrote an email to all the heads of school asking them to step in and they all told me to get over it.

Of the boy who took his own life after school ended, Ellie says: "He was friends with the bullies. I think he might have battled depression and just hung around to keep up."

Ellie's replies are a shock: this information, if true, is new. (I have not been able to verify it with other parties.) But it helps give me a deeper understanding of Vic's situation and find a more truthful narrative. Until I learnt this, I had put most of the blame on myself, my bad mothering, call it what you will. But as time has passed, Vic's fellow students such as Ellie have matured, and have been able to give me the information I need to hear. I also find it heartening that Ellie took a stand against what was happening, and I take comfort from how much Vic was clearly loved by her friends. They understood and supported her—but were failed by the school system.

Ellie: I was happy with my [own] classes—everyone in IB was a lot nicer so it wasn't as bad. I just avoided sitting downstairs. My friends and I would sit in classrooms during lunch and such.

Me: I think Vicky did the same thing.
Ellie: Yeah, the cool kids would take over the eating areas. It was isolating to go down there. It was a very toxic atmosphere and I even went to the counsellor at school. And she would complain about the teachers' actions or the students but she couldn't do anything.

All schools have popular kids and kids who are on the outer. However, most schools would, I imagine, take action when a student makes a complaint to a head of department. And what sort of teacher would pick on a child such as Victoria, who has attention deficit disorder and can't speak up? One who is ignorant about learning disorders, clearly. One who lacks empathy. And one who is pretty desperate to be liked by the popular bunch. So, one who is insecure as well. I'd like to think that eventually someone above him would have called him out, but no. This teacher has gone on to a job teaching at a prestigious private school overseas.

I wonder if another factor in the bullying, as described to me, was the status-consciousness among students at the school—fuelled, it must be said, by some parents. Malcolm and I did not have a car, a fancy apartment, or high-flying international careers with multinational companies, none of the status symbols that make social acceptance possible in an environment such as the school's.

We did not fit in, but Singapore's public-school system was not really open to us either. That system is—understandably—geared towards local kids and the specific needs of Singapore. One aspect is a huge emphasis on exam success, especially in science and maths. Foreigners looking for an all-round, less compartmentalised and streamed education, or one for which they didn't have to fork out a fortune, had little option but to put their children into one of the numerous international schools that had sprung up.

Many expats had salary packages that covered school fees, so private schools were an inevitable part of their lifestyle. For us, though, it was a struggle to pay the fees as we were employed on local terms. We were working in Singapore because a severe consolidation of the media industry in New Zealand meant there were few jobs available there.

The private school thing became a series of humiliations for us, the "non-expats". The Australian wives were cliquey and liked to cluster with their friends, although the same could be said of many other nationalities. They were in Singapore for a fun time. They went out together in tight groups in the evening to the bars downtown, or flew off to resorts to live the life, as they put it.

After Vic became a teenager I stopped going to the school whenever possible to avoid the glammed-up mothers with their broods of loud confident children. In the safety of their protective groups, it was easy to treat outliers such as me as oddities to be put down or made fun of. Once, I arrived at the school in the afternoon hot and sweaty as the trip there took two bus rides from my work. The mother of one of Vic's classmates drew me aside into the parents' room off the main corridor and said, "Don't tell me you caught a bus here. I am the wife of a CEO. I didn't come here expecting to have to mix with the likes of you."

In hindsight, it's hard to believe anyone would say something so vacuous and vicious. But I was tired from the journey, and by the time I had taken in what she'd said she'd gone.

My own insecurities probably prevented me seeing any unpleasant realities in the lives of these women. They may have had their own loneliness and frustrations, for which a life of seeming fabulosity was no compensation. All I knew was that in the corridors of the school and at parent-teacher evenings they excluded me, and their children, with a pack mentality, were in turn mean to Victoria, perhaps sensing her vulnerability.

As for how Victoria slipped through the net of the student welfare team at the school and failed to get the help she needed, eventually I get enough distance to rationalise what happened. A private school is a conglomerate. Like a company, it may have fantastic employees—teachers and other staff members—who are inspirational and everything you would wish for in someone to help your child learn. But, as with any company, there are also weak links. Mrs C was one of these.

I speak to Patricia to gain some perspective from her experience as a counsellor in private practice. She sums it up by saying that unfortunately Victoria had an inexperienced counsellor who didn't seem to have a safety plan. We will never really know what Vic told Mrs C as we will never get to see the full notes, Patricia points out. She goes on to explain that usually, when you are a counsellor and someone comes to you with suicidal ideation, you assess the risk. Has the person tried to kill themselves or self-harm? Do they have a plan? How often do they feel like this?

If there is any chance they regularly think about killing themselves, you create a safety plan. This is essentially an agreement they will not do anything to harm themselves or other people. They identify two people they will contact before they do anything rash. You print out the agreement, get the person to sign it, give them a copy, and also keep a copy in your notes.

If the person doesn't agree to sign such an agreement, the counsellor cannot let them leave as this would be a breach of their ethical code. The counsellor must intervene if a client gives them cause to believe they will hurt themselves or others.

In none of the case notes we received from the school was there a safety plan.

One day I would like to track down the mothers of the worst of the bullies. I would like to ask them if they knew about it, and is their child happy that they helped drive Victoria to kill herself and so render our lives irretrievably devastated? I wouldn't say it in an angry way. I wouldn't get hysterical. But they should have to face and experience something of what I am going through. It would be good to call them to account, even if nothing much tangible resulted from it.

But that is still far too measured, too rational. I want to be a bad mourner. Grieving people are meant to be meek and mild, humbled by death. They are always being comforted, always seeking a shoulder to steady them. They are stoic and noble, and then they move on with dignity. That's what the world wants.

I wish I could relive Vic's funeral again, to force the people there to see naked grief. Mourning unplugged. A maniacal mother springing out of a grief box. I see myself strutting into the funeral service in a red mini-dress, make-up applied so violently that my scarlet lipstick is a smear across my face, my hair alarming in a B52 beehive. I stand at the lectern and tell them all to fuck themselves. I point to the prefect bullies sitting awkwardly in their uniforms and accuse them of murder. And then I point to the parents and teachers and scream at them that they have blood on their hands, that their shallow values are a travesty of humanity. And then I throw myself shrieking and howling into the coffin and lie beside Victoria, only to be hauled out snarling, kicking and biting by shocked fathers, who step up with brute strength to manhandle the madness, while trying to avoid brushing with death.

Try and forget *that*.

27

STARING INTO THE ABYSS

I do not want to accept that the laptop journal is the most I can ever hope for in terms of getting Victoria back. A darkness begins to enter my heart. I am drawn to the hill near where she died, walking alone, retracing her last steps. I start to see a shadow out of the corner of my eye. It's a small trapezoid shape, completely black, flitting just within sight. When I turn, it is gone. I feel that it is evil and wants to enfold me.

I find myself returning once more to the block where Vic jumped. This time there is no voice directing me, unlike when I went there the month after she died. I have returned several times since. Gradually, as the months turn into a year, I have ceased to expect any uplifting message. Yet I go. My heart starts beating faster and I want to turn away, but something draws me on: I have the strength now to want to know more about her death.

I catch a lift to the tenth floor. I imagine Vic doing this prosaic thing of pressing the lift button. Did she look at her reflection in the lift mirror and adjust her hair, or mouth back to herself, "Goodbye"?

I go to what must have been the spot from which she jumped. I realise now that the point she reached is not at the top of the building, but at the common area around the final floor of apartments. Technically, it is the eighth floor, not the tenth, since the first two levels are basements. Vic must not have included the basement factor in her calculations—she probably just went off the list of floors in the lift. (The maths thing!) More or less instantaneous death is not as certain from that lower height.

One part has a ledge with a railing. I look down to the tiled entrance of the block and the carpark at ground level. Perhaps for Victoria it was like being at the top of a mountain, looking down at a world that appeared insignificant. It takes a special person to be at ease with heights, to want to climb up and up. The air is different up here, purer. Thoughts can float and rise.

I am drawn to the edge, even while resisting it. The wind whistles. I am discomforted but find some consolation—a kind person has left a single artificial red rose here. Right where my daughter had leant over that last time, it is there, tied on with string.

I imagine Vic taking off her sparkly flip-flops and placing her phone next to them. Neat to the last. I peer over the edge and count ten seconds—one for each floor—and then realise I should count eight. I wonder what the moments of decision and action are like. What final impulse caused Victoria to not only let go and fall, but to manage to land precisely on the tiny tiling area below? Any deviation to right or left and she could have landed on cars, or crashed through a gap next to the building's support pillars, down into the basement. I marvel at how she managed to land on her back, keeping her lovely face intact.

Did she change her mind and reach out to desperately try and stop her fall? There is a scrape mark down the side of the concrete. Or did she make the mark pushing away from the wall to ensure she landed precisely on the tiles? Is that how she broke her neck?

I look down to the little square tiles, so far but then not far, trying to imagine what it would be like to be broken and alone there. A child should not die alone.

And I try to be with my daughter in her death, even now. I force myself to feel Vic colliding with the tiled concrete with a whoosh and a thump, the bones and organs broken and crushed, the skull containing that restless racing brain, smashing like an egg. Did she cry out or moan or gasp or call for Mum? Was there a teenage, regretful, "Oh shit"? I think she probably shrieked. Did a startled kingfisher in the tembusu trees nearby shriek in reply? Was that the last sound she heard? Did she feel the blood? Were there moments of pain, or minutes?

Or perhaps the fall itself didn't matter in the overall course of things. I remember how I woke up that morning, with Victoria telling me in what I thought was a dream, "I'm free, I'm free." Was there a soul already rising and escaping from the cracked body, wanting me to know that the essence of Victoria was free, free at last from the horrors of a physical being in an earthly life? I look down, and still don't understand. But at least I have tried to fall with her.

28

DISSOCIATION

Vic herself had already rehearsed the experience. There is a short story in her laptop journal of March 19, 2014, filed at 02.18.

Dissociation
By Victoria McLeod

She sweeps over me. A shadow enveloping my consciousness. A feeble creature that clings to the dark to hold on. She survives only by the prospect of death being an entity that can be controlled. Suicide is her comfort blanket and I am her host. Her whispers invade my thoughts like a virus, manipulating them, directing them to her own operations. I capitulate. I let my defects turn into an unbalanced fulcrum, too far on one side to pull back to the centre.

I'm falling. She's me.

I am nothing. An insignificant cognisance. Incompetent. Fake. I know this and nothing can change my mind. Nothing. I let my thoughts roll over one another like restless waves, each one colliding and crashing on to the shore, dispersing into white foam and dissipating. Retreating and forming, calibrating themselves, over and over again. I need to do it.

But I can't summon the energy. I'm paralysed. What if I just sit here and rot? The thought sticks. I sit here and allow myself to drown in the thoughts I created which have now been etched with blunt knives into the threads of canvas that is my brain. I visualise looking over the edge. The ground is so low, yet I wonder if it's low enough. Is it possible to will your thoughts to overcome instinct? I have no choice. Thoughts have the power to destroy you. I feel a sudden rush of clairvoyance. I am on the ledge. Heart pounding like crazy, my whole unbroken body shaking like a leaf. I have never felt fear worse than this. This is not dread, it's adrenaline. The finality of this moment makes me slowly breathe in and out. I have no last words, no note. Just a prayer. My first and last prayer to an invisible divinity: that I will die.

I will forget that my bones will shatter, my heart will stop beating, my blood will rupture through a network of capillaries and arteries, my limbs will crack; bent in opposite directions; a repugnant, detached jigsaw puzzle. And I will fall like a book dropped from the top of an empty stairwell that lands with deafening jolt on a concrete slab, penetrating the silence.

Breathe in, breathe out. Close your eyes. Clench your fists. Fall.

I open my eyes. I'm on my bed. Could have sworn I had done it. No. It was my imagination. A useless fantasy fabricated as a cry for help. I'm still numb. It's raining. Blundering sounds on my roof. I forgot to turn on the light.

The rain somehow pulls me up out of bed. I walk with neither purpose nor aimless meander. I open the front door and walk out, aware that I'm still in my pyjamas; ludicrous cupcake patterns on scratchy cotton. The shirt too small and the pants too big.

I climb down the stairs outside. Raindrops blanket me. Weightless, colourless paint. I expected it to wake me. Snap me out of it. Stop my mind playing tricks on me. I'm stunned by the rain's persistence in crashing against my skin. Its simultaneous lack of permeating it. It's like I'm wearing several layers. Making me resistant to feeling. Anything but this strange, dazed dejection from reality. From happiness. Stupid word. No meaning. Childish.

I walk to the end of the road. The cars are luminous obstructions that do not hinder my way. I am done. Finished. I don't know what to do with this body, this parasite I am dragging around. This mind that won't leave me. I'm soaking. My hair hanging; a wet curtain. I don't care. I sit down, my back against a tree. Bark splinters pinch my back. I don't feel them. I don't feel anything. I am a weak animal in the rain, waiting to be saved. But the only person who can save you, is yourself.

I will never be saved.

ADJUSTMENT

II

29

HOW NOT TO ADJUST FOR LOSS

> Here are my things to sort out: ... The cash from my college fund that my parents spent years saving up, be spent on a nice trip. A break they deserved to have a long while ago.
>
> —Vic's journal

The idea of going on a "nice trip" after Victoria dies by suicide is monstrous. Utterly grief-stricken, we are hardly in any mental state to head off to sightsee the Loire Valley or loll around on a beach in Bali. But as days turn into weeks, months and years, life has to have more purpose than working and missing Victoria. But what? Coming to terms with a new life without our daughter and living it effectively proves a journey of mistakes, diversions, and good intentions gone awry.

Patricia had warned me: "Beware of filling the void with an impulsive I-need-to-feel-better-at-the-moment action. Beware of filling the void quickly without considering the consequences."

Malcolm and I miss being parents. One of our first impulses is to investigate adopting a child. I don't see this as filling the void or replacing Victoria, but as giving us purpose. Initially, we are told by a government official that it is possible for us to adopt a Singaporean child. The research, form-filling and interviews take about two years. When we are eventually approved, there has been a change of policy. We are informed there are no children available for us, nor is it likely there will ever be.

We also look into fostering. After months of form-filling and interviews, we learn we are not suitable because Malcolm at sixty-one is too old. There is also a question mark over our parenting on account of our daughter dying by suicide. This is intimated to us by a social worker, who takes pity on us in our bewilderment and our need to love a living child. She means well. It is good she told us.

It is understandable there would be doubts about us. Suicide can be seen as a rejection by the person of those around them, or as revenge for some perceived wrong. I don't think this was the case for Victoria. She wrote in her journal that she had had a happy childhood, that there'd been nothing "wrong" in her life. Still, we had failed to notice her deep unease. We had failed to have any inkling of her suicidal ideation. Malcolm and I agonise over these shortcomings.

Vic would probably be horrified by this ramification of her death. Then again, perhaps she would not have wanted another child to displace her in our hearts. I console myself with this thought.

A year later I receive a text out of the blue asking if we are still interested in fostering, and that there is a child who might suit. By then we are too exhausted and defeated to even reply.

For a while, leasing a black BMW at a vast monthly cost fills the void. I rationalise that we have no one now to save up for, so we may as well spend our money. At first there is pleasure in enjoying the surge of power from a well-engineered machine. I further justify it by thinking, *Vic wanted us to have a car*. But as Malcolm prefers to go to work by bus, where he can sit and text and take photos on his phone, and I often work from home, it is an indulgent luxury.

I upgrade to business class on a trip home to New Zealand. *I'm doing this for Vic*, I think. *She would have wanted me to treat myself.* The airport lounge access, priority queueing and fancy food and wine mean little to me. It is only sleeping on a lie-flat bed that has any appeal.

I spend more than I should on clothes and jewellery, and continue to buy stuff for Victoria, even though she is dead. It is a way of maintaining a connection with her. Silver jewellery that does not suit my olive skin colouring lies unworn in a drawer. A recklessly purchased $300 blouse with an unflattering blue and orange floral design reproaches me in my wardrobe. I suppose I thought Vic would have liked the flowers. But *orange*? She would not have liked that at all.

Malcolm racks up a $15,000 credit card bill in the space of four months on online purchases made late at night. He does things like buying the same CD and movie twice.

I tip wait staff overly much and sometimes hand out ten-dollar bills to strangers on the street who look needy. I contribute frequently to masses for the dead and church charities, not out of any considered concern for others but to feel good about myself.

Spending on health increases. I have bronchitis for a year. Malcolm has cancer scares. Tests include colonoscopies and out-patient treatment. I sprain an ankle falling down steps and it takes over a year to heal. Pain flares in Malcolm's collarbone, which he broke in a cycling accident when Vic was little. He had been doubling her on the crossbar and her shoe had caught in the front spokes. She broke a bone in her foot, which meant the end of ballet lessons.

An old back problem I've had, involving a sciatic nerve, resurfaces. During tennis coaching, Malcolm hurts tendons in his wrist badly and cannot play for months. We both have dental problems. Malcolm tries, and is unable, to quit smoking. Our consumption of alcohol increases. I start grief counselling sessions, which continue sporadically to this day.

―――

A study has found higher mortality rates among bereaved parents within the first three years of a child's death, particularly when the death is from an unnatural cause such as suicide. The same study also found that bereaved parents experience a higher rate of marital disruption than non-bereaved parents. At first Vic's death brought Malcolm and me closer together. After more than two decades in a de facto relationship, we got married at Singapore's registry office six months after we lost her. It felt right. I wanted to have the same surname as Victoria and so became Mrs McLeod.

After two years, our grieving takes different paths. Malcolm throws himself into his work and derives much comfort and needed distraction from it. I, on the other hand, find my newspaper work lacks a sense of a higher purpose. I want to make meaning from Vic's death in a way that helps both me and those in some sort of need. I have also felt lonely at home, with Malcolm away working nights during the week. We are still together, but it is hard.

Adjusting for the loss of a mere object such as a house in an earthquake should have been straightforward by comparison. While I felt sad that our house in Christchurch was wrecked, my main concern was not to lose the money I had put into purchasing the property. I wanted the insurer to honour my policy and either build me a replacement house or compensate me financially. The insurance term is "adjusting for the loss". It is strictly an accounting term. And to do this, the insurer has someone called a "loss adjustor". In some ways I envy them. It reduces the process to a clear, linear progression leading to an outcome measured in terms of financial calculation.

I hire a lawyer to try and sort the mess with the insurer. I tell him I can't think straight when dealing with the loss adjustor as I am grieving the loss of my daughter. He writes in an email: "In light of your current mental health, we need you to tell us how we can best assist you—this will minimise the risk of you being so upset by our correspondence."

"Current mental health"—the implication is that my grief is a temporary blip that has unhinged me for now, but which can be treated. And that grief is a mental condition, something not normal. Time heals. Get some counselling.

Or cheaper, just take drugs.

But grief can't be cured, even though it can be diverted for a while. It is not an illness. Grief is an extension of love, and if you loved your child you can't stop loving them and therefore you can't stop grieving. You can take drugs or go on drinking binges or throw yourself into your work, but the grief will lie there, waiting until there's an opening, and it will hit and pummel you with insistent and conflicting messages: "She's gone! She's not gone! She's gone gone gone. No. Yes."

30

STATES OF GRIEF

Mechanical work such as editing, with its intense concentration on the words of a newspaper story on a screen, helps break my cycle of dwelling on grief. And a year and five months after Vic's death there is a huge distraction: Singapore's general election, September 9, 2015. It is the first general election since 1959 that Singapore's founding father Lee Kuan Yew is not contesting. He died five months ago.

The ruling is uncharacteristically apprehensive. Will the populist mood of Brexit extend into the little corner that is Singapore? The opposition Workers' Party has made the bold decision to not just contest its single, stronghold constituency, but two others as well.

My thoughts will be totally focused on *The Straits Times'* coverage of this momentous day. No living in the past. I arrive to find the newsroom orderly amid the chaos. This is reassuring. Stories to copy-edit are not in yet, so I concentrate on researching the mood of the people via live videos from reporters on the ground, reporters and supervisors in the newsroom, and the curtain-raisers of other media.

As the early results come in, an air of disbelief permeates the newsroom. Whether rookie reporter or old hand, everyone is stunned. Polling station after polling station shows a huge swing to the People's Action Party. By the end of the night they have scored a landslide victory. The ruling party remains firmly in control. Voters have not caught the Brexit bug.

Editors are all smiles. There will be no disruption to Singapore's political cosmos, and so no ripple effect on the media that reports on it. There is a complicated relationship between the press and the government in Singapore, involving a mixture of control, fear, negotiation and self-censorship. It works for them, whatever Western critics might say about democracy and free speech.

As for me? It's not my party, not my country. I am just doing my job. This involves editing stories on the poll results, not just doing tedious line editing but getting the nuance right, working out the interplay of what is included and what is left out, being aware of political sensitivity and yet making a story connect with readers and capture the reality of the result for Singapore. And all as quickly as possible.

It is a long night but it has the appeal of a lack of emotion. Its main benefit is as a distraction, less opportunity for thoughts of Victoria to intrude. Yet they are lurking. As I stare at the computer screen after pressing

"Transfer" to send a story to sub-editors I find myself wiping away tears at the thought of Lee Kuan Yew, dead since March. LKY, as he is known (also, "the old man"): of all the people I could weep for, why this hard-hearted politician in a country not my own? Lee was a man able to negotiate with both the Japanese, when they controlled Singapore in the Second World War, and the defeated British. After a double first at Cambridge in 1949, which he never let you forget, he emerged to play communists off against more moderate anticolonial voices. This required a mixture of street smarts and extraordinary single-mindedness and self-belief.

This man, who led Singapore for fifty years of independence, said he would rise from his grave if things in the country looked like they were going wrong. Well, it has been five months and no sign yet of any sudden hectoring from an old and angry ghost.

Yet thinking of Lee as an old man, his powers to terrify and enthral diminished, envelops me in a terrible sadness. Why would I grieve for a man of entirely pragmatic vision, who appeared to have little empathy for the artists and illogical soothsayers of the world, as Vic once described herself? Lee maintained that encouraging cultural activities such as the arts could come only after the basic needs of a populace were addressed—taking care of the "rice bowl", as the local saying went.

Why am I sad? Vic was an artist with words who couldn't do maths. Lee would have had scant regard for her in terms of the economic value she could contribute to society. They did, though, share a love of trees. Early on Lee launched a tree-planting policy, and he took an interest in this right up to his death at ninety-two.

Vic and Lee had more than trees in common. Both had learning disorders. Vic's attention deficit problems affected her ability to process information. Lee had difficulty processing the written word. He found out later in life that he was dyslexic. By then, he had developed coping strategies and assumed everyone else could too.

Lee's beloved wife died, after being bedridden from a stroke for several years. Singaporeans learned of a soft side to their leader. Lee the devoted husband would read aloud to his wife nightly.

Why am I sad? Lee's death comes just over a month before the first anniversary of Victoria's death. She died April 2014; he in March 2015. In the run-up to milestones of any loss I find myself living with a constant undercurrent of dread. It's as if I am being dragged flailing and half-drowning through a waterfall. I become acutely aware of others' suffering, pulling me to the edge.

Just a week or so before Lee dies, Malcolm and I drive past the hospital where the old man lies gravely ill on life support. Malcolm wants to be near the action; news junkies are like this. Singapore General Hospital is in an unremarkable area of town, at the intersection of several main roads close to the city, surrounded by a mishmash of road markings, street signs and shopfronts.

A crowd has gathered outside the hospital. Flowers,

get-well cards, posters and even balloons festoon one end of this public area. I am gripped by the collective unconscious you feel in the waiting room of a hospital where a loved one lies ill. Life is on hold, breath is inhaled but not exhaled, all is suspended until the doctor's call.

We drive up a street lined with an umbrella foliage of rain trees, the physical manifestation of Lee's greening of Singapore policy. We make a U-turn and drive back past the hospital.

I realise one of the side entrances looks familiar.

The term "flashback" is overused. If someone says they have post-traumatic stress disorder, well-meaning people nod and remark, "Oh yeah, flashbacks." They tend to think of the disorder in terms of an on-screen trope, where a film cuts to the character's visual memory of a harrowing event. But on seeing the side entrance at the hospital, I am overwhelmed by sheer physical pain. It emanates from my heart: a muscle ripping apart, intertwined striations of flesh and blood and veins being stretched and pulled and torn, but clinging to their underlying structure, resisting the force of destruction.

Yet the source of this violent pain is not physical. It belongs to memory. I had forgotten that the entrance led to the morgue where Malcolm and I had been taken to formally identify Victoria's body nearly a year before. The trauma of seeing Victoria reduced to cold flesh and bone had altered the make-up of our cells at some chemical level. Our essence had got wiped. We had lost memory and cognitive function. We had lost a sense of purpose. Double helixes had lost their backbone.

A day or two after this harrowing experience, the old man dies. I find myself weeping constantly during the week of official mourning for a man I have never even met. I weep during the televised state funeral service, in which Lee's coffin is placed on stage during proceedings at the University Cultural Centre. (Vic had stood on that same spot a year and a half previously when she sang with a choir at her school's end-of-year concert.) I weep when the band plays the Singapore national anthem "Majulah Singapura" during the state funeral service. Victoria had known all the words, even though they were in Malay. I sob in the street or at my desk, and people think it is for their dead leader. Millions of people are weeping. I am sure many other people—normally those who keep their emotions under control, who keep a tight rein on display—weep for their own private losses, as well as for the loss of Lee. His death taps people's emotions at a deep level, even of those who hated him. The collective grief is comforting, liberating for them—and for me.

> Our words will be absorbed
> By the stars under your tembusu tree,
> And will be whisked away by the sultry squall,
> And forgotten in the morning.
> —Vic's journal

31

"SHE'S GONE, MOVE ON"

Starbucks has an outlet in a suburban mall close to where we live. I haven't dared return here until now. The thought of it makes my mouth drop into my heart—it's a feeling of unspeakable hurt and yearning. We used to go to this mall a lot. It was where we spent our little ordinary lives, which I now know are precious, even in their mundanity. It was where Victoria spent her last day and where she bought me a kaya waffle from the basement food court. She'd even dutifully returned my library books.

"I could go to Starbucks like every other normal boring person," Vic had written in her journal. She and I rarely hung out at Starbucks together, but it was a place to meet after we had done our separate stuff. If we ran out of coffee beans at home, I would get her to go there on her own to get us a packet. Malcolm liked Colombian beans, but Vic and I preferred the more mellow taste of "House" brand.

Epigram of Bitterness
She felt like she'd swallowed a bad cup of coffee.
Not the over-sweetened nutty-bodied kind or even the
acidic, granular fake kind that tastes like contaminated
water. It felt like an austerely bitter Colombian brew,
so acrid it burns the roof of your mouth and makes
you sick to your stomach.

—Vic's journal

But I'm here now. From my hard, uncomfortable seat—just a little too small for my frame—I can see the shiny packs of House and Colombian coffee beans on the shelves. The acidic taste that Vic disliked makes me feel connected to her. How can Malcolm drink that? Taste buds dulled by cigarettes, I suppose.

I've ordered a milky latte, for old time's sake. I usually take only a pared-down long black since Vic died. I am with an earnest young man, a fellow Kiwi who has offered to meet up at this mall—his choice, not mine—and toss around some "advice" on what I should do next. Strangers I encounter often go on to ask to meet up this way—"to chat", as they put it.

Perhaps it makes them feel good. They are moved by my story and want to help. Or they feel that my loss vindicates their own parenting skills, that they are an authority. A couple of times with expats it turns out they have suffered the loss of a loved one—not a suicide, but the death of an elderly father or mother—and for the first time in this alienated Singapore society they have someone they can unburden themselves to, and have a quiet weep. As for me, I'll give anything a shot if it helps me live another hour. Hearing someone say my daughter's name out loud is sometimes all it takes.

I met the man across the table at an information evening for people interested in adopting a child. He and his Singaporean wife have three kids of their own but are looking to adopt some from Africa. He says people respect you more if you have a big family.

I have agreed to come today out of curiosity. This man—a computer expert—is somewhat absent in the empathy department, so I know he will give me advice I don't want but need to hear. I am grateful for this. I can't thank him enough. Few people give me actual straight talk. I need a benchmark of ruthless pragmatism, if only to reject it.

Without preamble, he declares, "You have to accept she is dead." He doesn't make eye contact and is possibly on the spectrum. A nerd with an intensely logical, linear mind.

"What is she, your daughter? She is just bones. There's no such thing as soul. She is gone."

He swipes the air with a hand. The fluff of a cappuccino clings to his lips. An image of the wisps of tiny termite wings on our living-room floor comes to mind.

"That part of your life is gone," he says. He has three children and a wife who loves him. He shows me the photos on his mobile phone. He says they are all coming to the mall to meet me.

He is a lucky man. His life philosophy has served him well, I can't deny it.

"It's kinda exciting. You can create a new life for yourself," he goes on.

This is brutal but I can see the sense. He says something about discarding what doesn't make you happy, identifying what does, setting goals, achievement follows. Don't look back.

I'm so nice. I keep smiling. He's reaching into his back pocket to give me a business card. "There's this terrific organisation. Yes, it costs a lot to join. But they have these crazy intense workshops. You connect with likeminded people focused on maximising a great life."

I look over to my right, to tables at the back. There's an empty one. It's her seat. I know it, from out of nowhere. I remember a neighbour, an older Singaporean who often goes to the mall's food court for dinner, telling me that she sometimes saw Vic at a table at the back of Starbucks (after school on Thursdays or Fridays, when I worked late), writing or studying or reading. In fact, she saw Vic that Friday of the last weekend of her life, sitting here with her earbuds in, reading a book. Vic had smiled at her.

> I want to go to Forever 21 with X. We would parade around in high heels from New Look, and then go to Dior and pretend to be rich; trying on glamorous

> dresses we could never afford. Then go to Victoria's Secret and splurge on perfume. And perhaps try on some lingerie and have a sneaky kiss in the changing rooms. Then of course, go to Starbucks and get my notorious white chocolate mocha with whipped cream.
> —Vic's journal

I see Vic at that table, smirking at me as she puts down her cup of mocha sweetness. The cup makes a neat clinking sound on the saucer. "Mum, he's talking a load of crap," she would say. *Because love endures, you silly computer man,* she would call out, removing her earbuds, her words silencing the hubbub for a moment.

It endures—Vic's love for whoever X was at that time, six months before she died. And Vic's love of me and my love of her endure in memory, and in other cellular-level ways.

My love may have been a burden to her. Perhaps she saw it as just annoying maternal fussing. She is free of that now. Nevertheless, it endures as a thing apart. If I were to discard my love for Victoria and forge a new life, it is not a life I would want. It would commodify my endless mother's love, cheapen it. I need to keep this love intertwined with both my head and my heart. If love is just in my head, a behaviour or value or quality to be accepted or rejected at will, it insults a certain depth of feeling. It denies the very chemistry of being.

So, the one thing I can do, to at least feel alive, is to keep nurturing that love for her.

Computer man's family turns up. He has sweet kids. I thank him and they go.

I decide to believe that all of Vic is not dead, and that "moving on" does not mean discarding her. My daughter will always be more than just bones in an urn. She did communicate with me as she lay dying at dawn, telling me she was free and was happy. She can communicate with me still.

32

REDISCOVERY

A month later we are in New Zealand. It is April 13, 2015, the eve of the second anniversary of Victoria's death. I stand outside our cottage at Kakanui, gazing at the sickle moon. It is a spot where Victoria stood many times, a sliver of blondeness and bright eyes caught by the slim light of the moon and the glowing remnants of sunlight on the ridges of distant mountain ridges. If she were here, she would be ticking off which stars are already visible. If she were here, we would be living our old lives. I would be inside, pottering about in the kitchen. Malcolm would be near Victoria, raising a camera to the last bits of light, trying to coax it into the lens.

I stand at that spot and beg Victoria to send me a message that she is still—somehow—around. I hope for a sign from the sky, even as my logical self dismisses such cravings. But then I see a far-off flash of light that hurtles downwards through the sky, then disappears. Just like that. A dissolution. It is the flare of something burning at great speed. I blink. A shooting star.

On my return to Singapore, I pick up Victoria's journal. It has been a while since I last looked at it. Her words make her come alive again.

> Facts.
> I squeal exactly like a mouse high on helium.
> I find it very hard to keep my hands still.
> I can touch my nose with my tongue (but I still can't roll it).
> I am a cat-person.
> My favourite colours are aqua and lavender.
> I am a Potterhead.
> My favourite movies are *Loving Anabelle*, *Inception*, *Gravity*, *Harry Potter*, The *Lord of the Rings*, *The Fall*, and *The Perks of Being a Wallflower*.
> My favourite desserts are chocolate soufflé or pumpkin pie.
> My favourite perfume is White Musk by The Body Shop (or Chanel No. 5).
> My favourite tea: Earl Grey.
> I only like salty or cheddar popcorn.
> I always eat food clockwise around the plate, starting with what I like the least, and ending with what I like the most.
> I hate talking to people, except my relatives, on the phone.
> My favourite dog breed is the red setter.
> My favourite cat breed is Siamese.
> My eyes aren't blue—they are blueish green.
> I am not into the whole zombie apocalypse thing.

Actually, Vic's eyes were not blue-green but blue-grey, the same as her father, his sisters, her grandmother and her cousin. The eyes of Nordic boatmen scanning iron-coloured seas for clues to weather, food or enemies as they crossed to the coasts of Scotland, where they put down roots around what came to be called the Isle of Skye, which we promised Vic we would visit one day.

The list reveals only what Victoria wanted others to know. It does not even hint at her hidden self. This is a self that was confused and somewhat ashamed of her sexual identity, of her insecurities and her struggles to fit in socially. Victoria was insightful about her social anxiety, researching it quite deeply for a seventeen-year-old. This led her to be tormented by how her brain was failing her in social situations, such as becoming unable to speak when teachers asked her questions. This was humiliating and led her to withdraw further into herself.

In her writing she referred to herself as two people, one in conflict with the other:

> I badly want to stop living this façade of a mentally stable girl with nothing to say, when she has everything to say because the voices are screaming at her day and night. But Vicky tells Victoria the results of telling would be far worse. "They won't understand," she says. "They will abandon you." I bow my head because I know that Vicky is true, unlike Victoria, who is a liar. I'm a liar, a dyke and a dramatic stupid bitch who is wishing her life away.

> But even so, I badly want to tell them, I wish with all my heart that I could.

I, too, wish with all my heart that Victoria could have told us. I will never really know why she didn't, why her instinct was to conceal rather than reveal. Why it was easier or at least preferable to die than to ask for help.

It's such a dramatic word: "abandon". "They", I suppose meaning Malcolm and I, would never have abandoned her. And Vic acknowledges that. She knew deep down we were incapable of such callousness. Yet why did part of her want to think of us this way? And her thinking is self-contradictory. On the one hand, "Vicky" tells "Victoria" she will be abandoned, that this is true and "Victoria" is a liar. Does she mean "Victoria" knows the idea of abandonment is wrong, a lie? The "I" seems to be Vicky, but in the last sentence the "I" seems to be the part of our daughter that still could reason and function rationally.

As I read more about the psychology of suicide and talk to people about mental health, I start to get a better picture. Victoria might write adamantly that "You DO NOT HAVE TO BE CRAZY TO WANT TO KILL YOURSELF", but for a human being who is healthy and young to kill herself in such a violent fashion involves dysfunctional thinking.

There is no doubt, with the benefit of hindsight, that

my daughter was deeply disturbed and needed medical intervention. As to what was the cause, I can only guess. Perhaps a chemical imbalance triggered by puberty; a genetic predilection to self-destructive thoughts and an inability to problem-solve issues; complicated neurological causes; or a combination of all these? With this knowledge, I look back on Victoria's quirks and eccentricities, which we were happy to indulge but which I now realise may have contained hints about the self she wanted to keep hidden.

I never grasped how much of a perfectionist she was. She could never congratulate herself on her achievements or rationalise that sometimes good enough is good enough. It nagged at her very core. Take this journal entry:

> When I was out yesterday with Mary and X we saw Jody. You know, one of those chicks that look like they have it all. Blonde. Lithe. Head-Girl. Top grades. Popular. The whole jealously wrapped-up package. I mean she was exercising, for heaven's sake. Walking down Claymore Avenue with $200 Nikes and a cloned training buddy, no doubt to the gym. It's kind of beyond me how someone can have their life so sorted.

It did not seem to occur to Victoria that Jody might have had her own problems. Counsellors of teenagers I have spoken to in Singapore have assured me that even the most together-looking adolescent may be hiding depression or anxiety. The counsellors have plenty of clients from wealthy families.

As a mother, it is painful to acknowledge the "bad" sides of Victoria, but it is important not to paint her as some sort of goody-two-shoes or, worse, a saint on a pedestal. Perhaps talking about her grittier side may help others in some way.

There was the lying. It started to be an issue when Vic was about seven and the school rang to say she had not attended after-school badminton. She told me she had pulled out of the activity earlier and the teacher hadn't recorded it. I went in with guns blazing to defend Vic, only to find out that this was untrue. When I presented her with the facts, she was adamant she was right. I gave her the parental lecture about actions having consequences, that we must face up to our mistakes and own them, that if you lie people will lose trust in you, et cetera. She held herself aloof as I spoke, as if what I was saying had no relevance to her.

I thought this would be a phase, but it turned out to become deeply embedded for the rest of her short life. She would lie about having done homework, about not asking an ever-amenable Malcolm for extra money when I had already given her some—and, in hindsight, about how she felt "happy" when really she wanted to die. Deception became a default way of operating.

Naïvely, I always hoped for the best. I always thought,

"Maybe this time Vic is telling the truth." Often the lies were ill thought out and easily spotted. What made it worse was how she tied herself up in elaborate knots when a simple, "Oops, caught me out there, Mum. Sorry" would have been a better course of action.

A teacher emailed me that she thought Vic, then fourteen, had plagiarised most of a history essay. When challenged, Vic was mortified: "I would never do that." She was adamant the essay was in her own words. When the teacher showed us the original material in a book, she invented a story about the essay being just her notes from books and that she had lost her real essay. I ranted and raged that such lying did not reflect well on her character, that she was better than that. To no effect.

I have since learnt from psychologists that there wasn't a moral aspect to her lying, that the ADHD brain tends to make up stuff to fill information gaps and create false memories that the person really believes to be true. It's not dishonesty so much as a coping mechanism. The child may be afraid of admitting they made a poor decision. Or, if they have low self-esteem, they may be lying to boost themselves up when trying to make friends.

I find it better to dwell on happier memories. Vic was kind and compassionate. She volunteered after school at Riding for the Disabled and at the Asian Women's Welfare League, where she would help disabled people draw pictures, or accompany them on outings to places such as the supermarket.

She would talk for hours with someone like Mary, who needed to be comforted. She was the person who, on her last full day alive on Earth, helped her dad do the shopping at the mall, and who noticed that I hadn't blended my concealer in properly on my face, and who gently knelt next to me and rubbed it with one of her beautiful fingers. "There, Mum, that's better."

She loved animals and was the one in our household who fed the cats and checked on their water. She loved dogs. We didn't want to keep one in an apartment, so she befriended a red setter called Caesar, who was taken every day, along with the other household dog, Juno, to a nearby park by a domestic helper. Vic had a particular rapport with Caesar. She taught him to sit and to come when called. She would walk him while the helper chatted with other Filipinas in the park. One day, Caesar was no longer there. The helper told us new neighbours had complained about his barking and had thrown him poison meat. He died at the vet's. Victoria and I cried. Years later, I realised this was a catastrophic anguish she had gathered into herself.

That's another thing not on Victoria's list: she was courageous. I'll never forget how, at fifteen, just a slight young thing, she kept cool during a riding lesson at Bukit Timah Saddle Club one dusty late afternoon. Her instructor, William Scorpion, was Singapore's Mandopop king. A passionate equestrian, he would give riding lessons before his evening singing gigs. Sometimes he would turn up stage-ready, complete with coiffed hair, and sparkly Elvis-style costumes.

On this day, Victoria was on a lanky, nervous ex-racehorse. It suddenly took fright and bolted. I've been on a bolting horse and know that once they get in a blind panic they are unstoppable. Vic listened to William's steady, clear voice giving commands about what to do. She sat deep in the saddle, pulled the horse's head up and kept it circling until it got tired and slowed down.

Then there was swimming. While Vic was not a strong swimmer, she was a fearless one. On holidays at Phuket, she and Malcolm would swim so far out to sea I couldn't bear to watch. They would freestyle out over the breakers, to where the sea glittered like fool's gold and where the currents could swing and surprise them and take them anywhere.

She was also a fearless driver. At fifteen she was already driving our rented car during holidays at Kakanui, even though she had not reached the legal age. Unbeknown to me, Malcolm would take her out; I would learn of the expeditions later. She and Malcolm would exchange looks and slowly the story would emerge of her doing wheelies around a holiday park at Gemmells Crossing near Ōamaru, or driving brazenly down Ōamaru's bustling main street.

The day before she died she reminded me of a school trip to Malaysia. "Mum, do you remember we were on a sailing ship? I didn't tell you, but it had a tall mast.

I went to the top. I was scared, but I jumped from the mast right down to the sea. The others didn't think I could do it, but I did."

She also recalled a Singapore Press Club outing: "Remember when we went to Sentosa and Dad and I did the zip wire, and we also did the bungee jump? Dad was so scared, but I wasn't scared at all." She had wanted me to know this: that she wasn't scared of heights and she wasn't scared to jump.

33

THE NEED TO BELIEVE

For a long time, I seek out Victoria in religion. Although I was brought up a Catholic, attending a school run by Dominican nuns, I am a lapsed one. When Vic was alive, we had little time for the spiritual side of things. Sure, we had values, and codes of behaviour, but we dismissed organised religion as too formal. I last took Vic to church when she was about seven years old. Our Sundays were sacred only in their devotion to family fun, bike riding, playing tennis, swimming and doing chores together.

But in this new, unwanted life I need a foundation to cling on to. I accept an invitation from a neighbour to attend their evangelical church. The congregation is very welcoming. There are a lot of enthusiastic young people. Accomplished musicians on a stage perform songs with a gospel theme to a rock beat. Large screens beam them to the vast gathering, who clap and sing along.

A few months previously, in another life, this mass worship and singing would have seemed laughable. Yet now it's a comfort. The songs roll by, one after the other, and ordinary-seeming families, decent people, mums and the dads who have worked hard all week at the office, and their kids, surrender themselves to the passion of the music, a passion to feel love and give it, and to belong and be accepted. I sway among them and sob openly, the tears pouring down my face so much that a handkerchief is sopping wet in no time, and people just let me be. It is an outpouring of public grief that makes me feel ashamed but emptied and calm.

The neighbour comes to my home once a week with lemongrass tea in a flask and lessons on reading the Bible. There are set pieces to read and homework. I find concentrating on the reading difficult. My fragmented mind can't take in much. The lessons include learning about basic promises that God made to Christians, such as assurance of salvation and assurance of guidance. After you do various readings, there are questions to answer, such as: Describe a situation in your life in which you are seeking God's guidance. I write: Seeking understanding of Victoria's death and choices. Q: List ways how you can trust God in this situation. A: Believe that she is at peace. Believe she is experiencing joy. Believe that He has allowed her to remain part of us and guide us under His watch.

There are also messages from Pastor Kai, such as this: "It is the mundane things in a relationship that prepare you for the crisis—to see Him when something happens. Truth is what anchors love. Love anchored in the truth gives you life."

However, I do not feel Victoria's truth, whatever it is, and I need to.

Another neighbour gives me books on Buddhism. A yoga-teacher friend Sue, who knew Vic from when she was little, writes: "Victoria was a fey girl. She straddled two worlds, one foot with you and another in a world of light, golden, divine. The pull of the two existences must have been, at times, the most challenging aspect of this life. Through the years, I have only seen her occasionally, sometimes at the supermarket, or at the bus stop as I am passing by too fast. Yet still, that air of 'temporary' was about her, like her shadow wasn't with her, and that she would soon catch up to it, and be whole again ...

"From the yogic perspective, all life is suffering. But while we can accept that, we must also find the joy, however fleeting it may be. Know that she is home, whole, and grateful to you for your love and care in her short time with you ... Her gentle soul will have taught you amazing things, about the world, and about yourselves. She has set you off to the world of self-enquiry, and that journey is many things. What a gift."

These are wise words, but I am at a different stage on the life wheel. All I know is that I am not content with memories, imagined voices and signs. For a while I attend Methodist services at a traditional church in the city, on the leafy hill of Fort Canning, where Malay kings and English colonisers have come and gone. The choral singing at the Methodist church is uplifting. The sermons are down to earth. And the Methodists are practical: they link me up with a children's home that needs volunteers to help with tuition. I end up helping out there for more than a year. But still, at the church, I do not feel Vic's presence.

I explore Islam with nice non-denominational German neighbours who move in next door, replacing the owners of the territorial cat. We arrange for a tour of a mosque located in Chinatown on a Sunday morning, followed by refreshments and a chat. I am struck by the young boys sitting cross-legged in front of a teacher, with the Qur'an placed on little foldable wooden holders. The boys' concentration is absolute. They have a sincerity that is missing from contemporary youth's wise-cracking self-referencing. However, Victoria remains as remote as the dust caught in the sunlight of the madrasa, stirred up by the young boys' bare feet as they bend forward, studiously repeating the words of the Qur'an.

In November 2015 I go to St George, an Anglican church. The singing is choral, traditional and beautiful, and the organist stirring, but it is not easy standing in the pews of the quaint brick church of St George on a Sunday morning. When Victoria was about three, I would bring her here once a week for a Tuesday morning mums-and-tots gathering. We went for about a year. The wooden pews at the front are the same as they were then. We would sit and sing along to jolly hymns, sometimes standing to mime actions with the songs—putting our hands together if there was a mention of prayers, pointing to the air above if they mentioned heaven, crossing our arms around ourselves at the mention of "God's love". We were such innocents, then.

The children loved these sessions. One day a well-meaning organiser let loose a bunch of balloons in the church to represent the Holy Spirit. The balloons rose above the pews, only to burst with a huge bang. Victoria screamed; it would mark the start of a lifelong fear of balloons. Sitting in a nearby pew, remembering the balloons, I long for that innocence.

Later, I go to one of Vic's favourite cafés at Tanglin Mall. There I meet up with a group of women, parishioners from St George, who include Jean Marshall, widow of Singapore's former chief minister, David Marshall. Jean advises me to try the hot chocolate. I don't tell her that Vic would come here specifically for it. "It's proper chocolate and not too sweet," she once explained.

Jean's very grown-up daughter is here from England and has purchased a pair of strappy, summery shoes from a shop upstairs. It's strange to see a mother and daughter interacting over this simple thing, to see the fondness. I had forgotten all that. It's a blessing to have a happy memory of Victoria parading up and down our living room in newly purchased buff-coloured boots, pushing back her long hair to peer down at them and say, "What do you think, Mum?"

Soon afterwards I have another session with Patricia, the grief counsellor, who is Catholic and the mother of adult daughters. She says Vic's death was not inevitable. "Even Christ said, 'My time has not come,'" she tells me. That is quite a powerful thought. I have never before seen a reluctance in the crucifixion narrative.

Patricia continues: "Vic became focused on that thought of death. Her mental anguish comes through in the writing in her journal. She had fears and worries about what lay ahead and saw it bleakly. But teenagers do this. They don't know. Importantly, in her journal Victoria is very rational and sane. It is her understanding of life—she is very true to her values—that would lead perhaps to her thinking her life is not worth living, although this was the wrong conclusion to make."

One Sunday morning I give a Catholic church a try. I look up bus timetables and go to St Ignatius church not too far away, knowing nothing of it. It turns out to have a Jesuit seminary and gardens dating from 1961, with the church building itself having been built in the 1990s. It is expansive, comfortable and air-conditioned. The congregation is a mixture of Filipina domestic helpers attending Mass on their day off and Singaporean parishioners, who include showbiz celebrities. I feel alone among the close knots of extended families and smiling Filipina women in their orbits of friendship.

I manage to avoid my solitary weeping until "Lamb of God, you take away the sins of the world." There is something about the innocent lamb imagery that does it to me. No one takes any notice as I dab at my face.

And yet, standing there, I hear Victoria's voice saying, *You'll be safe here, Mum.* A great peace comes over me.

Later, at home, I research St Ignatius online and discover a Bible study group that meets on Saturday afternoons. Their latest course, eight weeks of "A Walk with the Blessed Mother", has just started but there is still time to join. The title sounds over-the-top Catholic but I go.

A group of kind Singaporean women take me under their wing. It must be difficult for them to have this constantly teary person in their midst, stumbling over long forgotten prayers, and wanting to talk about her dead daughter all the time. Not to mention having in their midst this sole Caucasian foreigner, whose husband is an atheist. And yet they take me in.

Sessions are held in the two-storey Sacred Heart Hall, a functional building at the back of the church. At my first meeting we go to an upstairs meeting room to discuss a Bible reading on the Annunciation, when Mary was told she was to be the mother of Christ. There is a quiet, soothing simplicity to being in a room with a group of women offering prayer for others. The female ritual of some social situations—comparison, status markers, put-downs—is absent. I start to crumble inside and a little old Chinese woman with a kind face and rheumy eyes reaches over and grips my wrist. "Mother Mary" is all she says. But I know what she means. I am no longer unmothered.

Victoria had lacked a spiritual framework, or one

I was aware of. Perhaps for her own protection she needed one, to take her out of her own problems, to feel supported by a community, and to feel loved by God or a god or gods, or the universe for that matter. And to be protected from physical, emotional and spiritual harm. Instead, her main rite of passage in her short life was to be ushered into the domain of the dead. It is too late for me to protect her, but I can take on a spiritual framework as a torch to carry for her.

Religion is uncool among many young people. How do you give them a little faith? It is complicated for me by the fact that most religions have traditionally regarded suicide as a sin. If people view suicide as a sin, the logical outcome would be to see Victoria as in purgatory. However, numerous Christians have told me they believe Victoria is forgiven, as their God is forgiving of a young, unaware person and is merciful. One of the practical Methodists, the neighbour who used to see Vic at Starbucks in the mall, tells me she is quite sure that Vic is in heaven. I find this reassuring—not so much heaven, which is nebulous to me, but the idea that Victoria is in a place where judgement is no more.

I don't believe Vic had a fully formed intellect when she made the decision to take her own life. You need only read her journals to see her innocence, suffering, and beseeching for help. She repeatedly tries to pray for her despair to be eased, such as in this entry written one month and one day before she died:

THE NEED TO BELIEVE

She prayed and prayed,
The covers wrapped around her,
Listening to the clock tick away her time,
Until the day she left the bed,
And left herself behind.

34

HOW DO YOU LOSE A DAUGHTER?

How do you lose a daughter, and all your past as you understood it, and all your little hopes for the future? In terms of time, very easily, as it happens. One minute you are a family sitting on the sofa eating spaghetti Bolognese while watching a food programme on TV. Next morning there are just two of you slumped there crying.

Of course, people "lose" daughters all the time: they go off to tertiary study or move in with unsuitable boyfriends, or suitable ones. Or they go off for gap years overseas or to work in other towns. But losing one to death is final. The daughter is not just temporarily mislaid pursuing youthful self-discovery, just no longer a physical and emotional presence in your day-to-day life. She is never coming back. It's self-evident, isn't it? (No matter how much part of me will never accept she won't be coming back.)

Loss is something everyone experiences in some form, so well-meaning people tell me they understand what I'm going through. Their context, though, might be a tearful farewell after dropping off a daughter for her first year of university in a new town. I appreciate that their lives are therefore forever changed, that there might be grieving for the loss of an identity dear to them, such as their role as the mother raising children. But, even if they do not realise it at the time, they have new purposes and plans on the horizon—the proud parent at graduation, the mother of the bride, the grandmother. Their child has a new future and they have a role in that. But our teenager died and, what's more, in a way that left those left behind forever broken because it was her choice to die, to not have a future. So you wonder: what carelessness or fault or ticking time bomb in your raising of her caused you to lose her?

It is ultimately a pointless question in terms of a definitive answer, but I ask it anyway. I peer at every memory as if it is a precious stone, keeper of a secret that I can read if only I try hard enough. I'm not looking for blame or seeking forgiveness. I'm seeking a connection with Victoria, first. Even regrets over opportunities missed and events mishandled, marks that she indeed lived.

Was I depressed during my pregnancy? Could a mother's depressed and anxious state of mind seep into the womb, clothing the foetus in a chemical veil of tears? During my pregnancy I suffered anxiety and anger when a colleague at work tried to get me removed on spurious grounds from my job. Fortunately, other workers stood up for me and I was kept on. But it weighed me down, although I was also empowered by the person growing within me, glad I had created a life.

Perhaps Malcolm and I were not a great pairing for parenthood! For people in their late thirties and early forties we were quite immature. We had lived a self-centred, immediate kind of life. We were two introverted, arty New Zealanders who had moved to Singapore for media jobs.

There were warnings from some. My Singaporean female doctor said: "Congratulations, you are pregnant. But how dare you have a child outside of marriage?" She was the product of a more prudent, conservative society than we were, and Malcolm and I sniggered. But perhaps she had grounds to be worried. Consider who sat before her: Malcolm in Doc Martens and stove-pipe jeans and me in geeky specs and clownish red-striped tights, more bookish kid than woman in the prime of her life. "Not a natural mother," Malcolm's mother was to declare some years later. She didn't mean it in a particularly cruel way. She had been a matron at her local hospital in New Zealand for many years. It was an informed observation, albeit wounding. She was right—on a tour of the Singapore hospital where I was to give birth, the sight of rows of swaddled babies, all needy, sentient beings, overwhelmed me. I nearly fainted. I remember thinking with alarm: Malcolm and I are going to have one of these.

But then how many parents are "natural", especially

in this day and age, where academic subjects are taught, but not the skill of living: how to find the right attributes in a partner; how to raise a family; how to get a baby to latch on to a nipple; what sort of nappies to use.

Did we need more support than we realised? I looked forward to having my own family, we three against the world. I envisaged a child growing, a future stretching out over the horizon, a wedding, and perhaps grandchildren. My own life, validated.

The three of us—Malcolm, newborn Victoria and I—take a taxi home to the apartment, where our new lives begin. How we adore our little Victoria Skye Pringle McLeod. The name Victoria is Malcolm's suggestion, elegant and traditional. Skye, after the ancestral seat of the McLeod clan, and after a beautiful grey horse I once owned. That horse was my inner spirit, brave and fast. As the years passed the name "Skye" suited Victoria; she loved the night sky, the stars. She loved nature. Pringle was after a relative of Malcolm who had been killed in Italy in the Second World War.

I have no friends or family in Singapore to help. It's an unnatural set-up compared to how humans evolved to be small tribes that helped enable the long and complex process of raising children. Colleagues advise me to employ a live-in domestic helper, and into our lives comes Amy from the Philippines. Although she is unmarried and has no children, she is from a big family. She knows how to sing to a baby "Sayang, sayang", a Filipino and Malay term of endearment that roughly means "There, there, darling". It can also refer to waste, as in "what a waste these tears are". There is a sense of both love and loss.

I learn. I am grateful. I enjoy breastfeeding, I like to laugh with Amy. I am thankful that I can get some sleep. It is a shock to find I love being a mother, I like thinking of nothing but the present and the baby and looking at her asleep in her woven Moses basket on our bed. I could gaze forever.

My obstetrician advises that if I want to have another child I had better do it straightaway, given my age. But we get caught up in the here and now and forget this advice. We never do get around to giving Victoria a brother or sister. Perhaps that was a mistake. It's lonely, being an only child. Out of the blue one day when Vic is about nine, she says, "Mum, I wish you would adopt a sister for me. An Asian sister."

Perhaps Victoria developed long-term attachment issues when I returned to work? All I got was three months and two weeks of complete happiness—that is how little time my Singapore maternity leave comprised. I was never so fully happy again. At three months two weeks, it felt wrong to leave Victoria. I felt I was abandoning her. At three in the afternoon, when I headed off to work, a routine emerged of disappointment and puzzlement in Victoria's eyes, then loud howls. Eventually this became soft cries. I learnt to leave during Victoria's afternoon nap.

To a young, developing brain, did this absence of the mother develop neural pathways of longing or a primitive form of blame? Did this turn into a fear of absence that became a fear of abandonment? Victoria was always clingy with me, right to school age. She preferred the company of Malcolm and me to playing with other children. At work I would daydream about her beautiful soft hair and face, and her sweet milky smell. In between editing news stories, I would slip away to express milk in a toilet cubicle. It was a furtive act: back then not many mothers did this. A colleague asked if I fed my baby breast milk because it was cheaper than powdered milk. I explained how human milk was the best nutritionally, and how the act of breastfeeding was a part of bonding with your child.

"Bonding," he snorted. "A Western concept!"

I gave up trying to express milk. It was just all too difficult.

I tried to explain to baby Victoria that I was going away to work for her future, to acquire a house, to pay for travel to New Zealand, but all this nonsense was rightly beyond her understanding. I made the most of weekends, when we three went for afternoon walks along the tree-shaded roads of the estate where we lived. Victoria by now could get out of her pushchair. She was able to totter about on her own, drawn to the curious beauty of brown tamarind pods on the grass verge. She would run her fingers along their curved form and shake them to hear the seeds rattle.

The three of us would go shopping at the supermarket, where crinkled old women exclaimed at Victoria, stroked her forehead with their jade-braceleted arms and pinched her dimpled cheeks. I would make the most of the long mornings together before work, laughing as we watched a video of *Playschool* or *Bananas in Pyjamas*. Amy made sandwiches or scrambled eggs for lunch. We would eat together, Vic in a highchair, a *Straits Times* to one side, which Malcolm and I dissected in terms of news placement, the placement of photographs, headlines I would have rewritten. Vic would look on, laughing. I would make the most of the time when I got home late at night. If Vic woke up, Malcolm would put on a Moby CD and the three of us would dance together, holding hands and spinning.

However, as Vic grew the apartment block became too isolated. I was worried, too, that, Amy was becoming overly possessive of Victoria and she found work with another family. I cut back to part-time work and we moved to a condominium with playgrounds where Vic would meet other children. She began to go twice a week to a Montessori preschool.

An Australian family with three girls lived next door to us and the girls treated Vic like a sister. They played pretend games in a park downstairs, making mud pies and boiling soup in a "pot", stirring it with a twig. Vic also had a friend in another flat. This girl's parents came from Mumbai and Jaipur. She and Vic completed endless wobbling circles on their bicycles, their ponytailed hair tied up in pink ribbons, their ringing of bells chiming with their high girlish shrieks.

Should we have moved back to New Zealand? We had built our cottage in Kakanui because I wanted Victoria to have a strong connection with New Zealand. It was ten minutes from Ōamaru, where Vic's grandmother Sheila lived. Vic and her grandma had an instant rapport. They shared a love of flowers, of colours, of decorum and of being well read. We visited once or twice a year from Singapore, choosing to spend our money on this rather than buying a car and dining out.

Christmas Day was always wonderful. Vic's job was to set the table. The knives, forks, and spoons were precisely placed. Flowers for vases were selected, rejected, chosen again, until perfect. When Vic was twelve, Grandma Elaine taught her how to bake a pavlova. The meringue was perfect, crunchy on the outside, soft marshmallow on the inside. Added to Victoria's Christmas Day roles was that of Pavlova Queen.

But while she loved visiting New Zealand and experiencing Kiwi Christmases with family, Vic felt she did not belong there, or in Singapore. This is a problem faced by many children in an increasingly globalised world: they end up being raised somewhere that is not their home country. There's even a term for such children—third culture kids, TCK. Vic wrote about it poignantly in her journal: "I'm not a New Zealander. I don't care that it's on my passport, I am just not one. I don't know how to adapt. I would miss Singapore too much. But at the same time, I can't stay here. I don't think I'd ever really find anywhere."

In Singapore, the academic pressure began to pile on. Malcolm and I discussed whether we should move to New Zealand, where the educational structure was not all about academic grades, but also vocational training. But he and Victoria both hated change, and we gave up on the idea.

Vic enters adolescence and grows into a tall willowy beauty. I think this will gild her path in life. She is more beautiful and kind and intelligent than I could ever be. She seems a better version of the genes of her parents. She makes Malcolm and me feel that our lavishing of love and our sacrifices of time and money are for a greater good. She is a seventeen-year-old heartbreaker in skinny jeans and ankle boots, strutting into adulthood.

She writes in her journal:

> I have so many opportunities. If some people were me, they'd be so happy. They'd have their own room. They'd have a great school. They'd live everyday like it was heaven. Hence why I am being completely self-indulgent. I shouldn't be so wrapped up in my own stupid, worthless problems, when some people would

give anything to live my life. I have my whole life ahead of me. So why can't I just live it?

So why couldn't she just live it? Jesse Bering, an American psychologist and the author of *The Belief Instinct*, has shed some light on this in a new work on suicide. Informed by the work of social psychologist Roy Baumeister, Bering compiles a list of six errant beliefs that can set the mind into self-destruct mode. No. 1: "One of the more surprising things about suicide is that most people who kill themselves have actually lived better-than-average lives. An experience that to many of us wouldn't seem so bad, or at least certainly not something to end one's life over, to others is exaggerated. This is because that individual has unrealistic goals for their personal success, or their happiness has been hitched to an unsustainable star."

35

HELLO FROM THE OTHER SIDE

I begin volunteer work once a week, teaching English at a children's home. Right from the first session with girls aged between seven and eleven, I gain an inkling of just how dysfunctional Victoria was. It is a shock. These kids are from broken homes, they have lived unimaginable lives of disruption, and possibly one or two have even been abused, yet they are relentlessly cheery and enthusiastic. They are confident and forthright with each other. They read social situations quickly and know when it is better to duck away or go forward.

What's more, they are quick to understand their homework and are insatiable about learning new things, whether it's a new reading word or how to bake brownies. They fire questions at me, file away the knowledge, then display it later. They have tons of initiative, never having to be told twice to put away books or go to the maths tutor if he has arrived. Nor do they require intense one-on-one sessions. They like the attention they get from these but are also at ease in group learning. In fact, if I get too intense with them, they become uncomfortable. They want to know what they need to learn, and then get on with it.

Being with them makes me reflect more deeply on Victoria. She needed intense one-on-one help to do her homework. She wasn't confident and forthright with other children. She couldn't read social situations quickly when she was a participant, although as an outside observer she was astute. I had never realised these aspects of her because I did not interact much with other children in terms of observing them or have any knowledge of what was considered appropriate behaviour at various stages of development.

I am inspired to do a six-month night-school course on teaching speech and drama to kids.

All this opens my eyes to the fact there is a substantial number of any given population who have learning and/or social functioning problems, trying as best they can to get along in a world where the majority think much more effectively and quickly.

Victoria had taken a long time to walk. She preferred to crawl. It was about nineteen months before she took her first faltering steps. The usual time was twelve months. Even after learning to stagger around confidently, she wasn't a child who would dash off, or get lost exploring.

Ball games were difficult. Vic could shoot goals well enough, but often switched off during games and went into a dream. This upset her more competitive fellow players, and they began to exclude her. The worst experience came during her first season of netball, when she scored an own goal. I wasn't there, but she came home in tears. She must have been about seven. She had been so proud of wearing the uniform, of being in a team. The other girls had turned on her and she never went back. I phoned some of the mothers; they made it clear they thought she was a joke and did not want her back. There had been a change of organisers that year and netball had turned much more competitive.

She never did learn to tie her shoelaces properly.

These things were not a big deal to us because Victoria was so brilliant with language. She learnt to read from an early age and devoured books. Her speech was clear and precise and articulate. She could make clever jokes and understood irony. And there were physical pursuits she enjoyed. As well as swimming, she did ballet and passed her basic Royal Academy of Dance exams. And she went horse-riding. But while Malcolm and I did not realise it, the general dreaminess, the lack of concentration and the clumsiness *were* a big deal. As we didn't have other children and didn't mix much with other families, we didn't see this. We loved Victoria for who she was. Yes, an assessment had reported high signifiers of ADHD, but to us she seemed reasonably socially and academically competent.

ADHD involves processing issues. These are a huge factor in academic smarts and, more than that, in socialising and feeling good about yourself. If a person can't function well in the so-called "normal" world of academic achievement and in the whole school environment, their self-esteem suffers. They get excluded. This leads to a host of other problems, including hyperanxiety about the dreaded and all-important school exams of the final year.

We had shared the psychological assessment with the school, and the student welfare team had agreed to help Vic by, for example, sitting her at the front of the class and not making a fuss about her repeatedly dropping her pencil and fidgeting. The following year, another counsellor at the school (the earlier one had left) asked if we wanted to put Victoria on a drug such as Ritalin. Ritalin alters the balance of chemicals in the brain so the person has better control over their impulses.

The counsellor's inquiry was a surprise. We had no idea that Victoria might be in need of drugs to alter her behaviour. I asked Vic if she would take them and she was adamant she did not want to. She said it would dull who she was, and she did not want that. We went along with that.

Things must have got difficult for her at school after this. It had become an isolating place, where she felt inadequate. She hid this from us, telling only her diary. Her school reports showed her getting mostly acceptable and sometimes good grades. The one consistent complaint was that she was "shy", but we assumed that the knowledge of her ADHD was being passed on to all teachers.

I undertake a year-long diploma in learning disorders, studying on my nights off work. There are four modules: learning disorder management; speech language development; child psychology; and counselling. In the child psychology and counselling modules, some students are mothers of special needs children and they share the difficulties their kids face, such as being bullied in the playground or yelled at by uncomprehending teachers. Such children do not fit into the conventional school system, with its academic emphasis and rewarding of those who excel in that area.

We study how children with learning disorders get excluded at playtime. We learn that when they are around seven it really hits them that they can't keep up in the schoolroom either. This leads to feelings of inadequacy, self-doubt and lack of confidence. This can sink into self-loathing and self-harm.

As a result of this course I learn that Victoria probably had a host of problems we were not aware of. Most likely she was on the autism spectrum: she flapped her arms when stressed or confused and had trouble "reading" non-verbal communication, both classic signs. She was easily overstimulated visually and aurally and was acutely sensitive to smells: the smell of coffee and food on a plane made her sick.

This also explained that what we thought was procrastination was simply her inability to process what to do and how to do it. She got distracted all the time and was unable to refocus.

I suspect she also had undiagnosed obsessive compulsive disorder, OCD. I am more aware now of the compulsive nature of the hair-pulling episode but there were other signs as well. As a young child, Victoria would line up her Barbie dolls repeatedly in exactly the same order and position. As she got older, she developed an intense focus on precise folding of towels and sheets, and the living-room lights had to be turned on in the same order. This extended to eating food in the same order and sticking to the same routine each day.

A recent article in *Australasian Psychiatry* describes a young woman aged fifteen who had OCD and was simultaneously treated for ADHD. She was prescribed Ritalin and this helped treat the OCD, too. This points to both disorders having some dysfunctional behaviour in common. It might be a clue as to how Victoria became obsessed with suicide—what psychiatrists call "suicidal ideation". The OCD brain is wired to lock into repetitive ways of thinking—in Victoria's case it latched on to self-harm and suicide.

It also finds it hard to shift from such thoughts. Victoria could see that rationally her thoughts of suicide were illogical but could not rid herself of them. She was incapable of regulating her dysfunctional thoughts. In addition, self-harming made Vic feel good for a moment, so her disordered, repetitive- behaviour-seeking brain kept seeking that brief jolt of pleasure.

These are striking conclusions that fill me with

immense sadness. There was the beautiful, witty, articulate person, whose brain was at war with itself, wired for self-destruction. And, try as she might, there was not much she could do about it. Her condition required intervention, drugs, cognitive therapy and other behavioural rewiring, counselling, and possibly spells in psychiatric wards.

As an adolescent interested in counselling, Victoria read up on anxiety and knew about the pleasure of self-harming. She also understood about trying to create new pathways of thought. She wrote in her diary when she was about fourteen:

> I want to focus on exercising. I'm going to swim for half an hour on Mondays; do push-ups and stretches every day, go jogging on Wednesdays, do yoga as a CCA on Thursdays (with X and Y), and do contemporary dancing on Saturdays. Besides, we're supposed to do one hour of physical activity per day. Dieting and exercising will be like a goal I can work for and it will keep me distracted from all the emotional stuff, and when I do get frustrated at home, like from my parents and school work, I can turn to self-harming. It's not the normal thing to do, but I think it's the only way I can cope. And it does work temporarily, like I'm destroying something inside me.

These were not the only internal problems she was fighting. From my diploma studies, I think she probably had aspects of dyscalculia, an inability to recognise symbols such as those used in maths, and maybe dyspraxia, otherwise known as "clumsy child syndrome". She was late in walking and learning to ride a bicycle and took a long time to master the tumble turn at swimming, for example. Considering all this, she was remarkably highly functioning. She held it together for as long as she could. And then she couldn't.

It is late evening when the last session of the diploma course ends. Classes are held in a building in the central business district and it is easy to hail a taxi. The driver's radio is playing one of Vic's favourite songs, "Pumped-Up Kicks". I think of how Vic probably identified with the song's theme of social isolation at school, and of wanting to end it all, taking all the "normal" kids down with you.

It's a horrible theme, involving dysfunctional thoughts, but I understand the "why" a bit more now. And I feel a sense that Victoria is pleased I have come to that understanding and wants me to use it to help others.

I ask the driver to turn up the radio. He looks back at me, surprised. Passengers, especially older ones like me, don't usually make such requests for teen music like this. He pumps up the volume. We head down a road to a tunnel connecting to the expressway. It's a road I have travelled every Tuesday evening for a year, returning from the course. Every street sign and shop are familiar. I glance out and see a neon sign inside the window of a bar. I have never seen it before. In bright orange, it spells out *Hello from the other side.* Underneath it, bizarrely, is a smaller sign: *The Bell-Jar.* Sylvia Plath's book of this name still sits undisturbed on Victoria's bedside table, just as she left it.

36

SHRINES AND BOXES

It is December 2013, our last Christmas together, and Victoria's seventeenth birthday. Plans are being finalised to start the building of the house in Christchurch. On the drive from Kakanui to Christchurch to catch the plane back to Singapore, we call in at the architect's office. We want him to help us choose colour schemes, flooring and other features. It seems best to do this face to face.

Earlier, Malcolm and I have bought test pots and tried out various whites along a paling at Kakanui. I do not like any of the shades of white, grey or beige. Vic is the only one in our household who fully grasps how colours work. She hasn't liked any of the test colours either. But when we pull up at the architect's office, she refuses to come in and help. She folds her arms and turns her face away. She wants no involvement in the house.

Malcolm and the architect eventually manage to persuade her. She looks at paint charts and brochures with enthusiasm and chooses the colour scheme—an exterior of a warm beige called Half Cloudy, a roof of Grey Friars with titanium trim, and interior walls of white with an undertone of yellow/green, adding a lightness. She goes on to choose vanilla oak plank flooring for the living room, grey and white flecked wool carpet for the rest of the house, beige porcelain Spanish tiles for bathrooms, and oyster-coloured drapes and blinds with a floral pattern of soft French blue and beige.

Two years later, the builder phones us to say the house is nearly built. It will stand as a repository of Victoria's style. Or, rather, a memory of it.

However, when we fly from Singapore to see the house, it is not ready. The basic structure is complete, but there is no replacement fourteen-metre-long retaining wall to stop the road and parking bay above from falling on to the house. There are no steps around the house and, worse, no steps from the road down to the front door. The only access is a makeshift plank of wood the builders have used. I discover this only when I visit the site. We have a beautiful box on the side of a steep hill, and no safe way to get in the front door or walk around it.

Months later, after much fuss and consulting of lawyers, all construction, including the retaining wall and entrance steps, is finally complete. By the end, the loss adjustor and the builders are not on speaking terms. The insurer has even hired another construction firm to build the retaining wall. I will never find who left vital parts of the build off the scope of work, or why it took years to remedy this. The only person who probably knows the full story is the last loss adjustor, whom the insurer brought on board just a few weeks before Victoria died.

Jackie (not her real name) had a reputation for being brought in to resolve "difficult" cases such as mine, involving parties in dispute. I was warned her style involved browbeating claimants into a state of submission through sheer bamboozlement. Indeed, she confused the lawyer I hired, who engaged in endless emails with her until I had to end his services, five thousand dollars the poorer and no further ahead.

I doff my hat to Jackie, who was ruthless in pursuit of damage limitation for the insurer. The house did cost the insurer nearly four hundred thousand dollars over its initial lowball offer, but it could easily have ballooned to several hundred thousand more. Jackie was successful in obtaining closure on a project that had dragged on for years. She was just doing her job as part of the corporate machine, but it was upsetting to be hugged by her at a site meeting and told a kereru flying above us was the spirit of my dead daughter blessing us. On other occasions our reasonable inquiries were fobbed off, and requests for works accepted, then refused.

After the house is finally completed, I look up Jackie on Facebook. Loss adjustment—of the actuarial type—is certainly her forte; she posts publicly that she is having "a wee wine and quality time with myself" at a resort.

There is "a cruise to look forward to, and a nice big payday at the end of the year".

For me, there is no neat sign-off. I try to draw up a spreadsheet analysing the insurer's costs and my costs to have the house built. The removal and addition of figures over several years of calculation and recalculation become an overwhelming blur.

I wish my calculations were a poem, something I could relate to. But they are the plodding realm of bookkeeping. I type them up and dutifully place the document (one of about twenty holding documents to do with the insurance claim) in a blue ring binder labelled "Total expenses for house". The costings involve a dogged, decidedly non-creative accountancy, a logical progression, a toting up of sums, an offsetting of loss and gain, evoking at some level what insurers term "loss adjustment", in essence what it costs them to adjust their financial reserves to compensate for your loss.

Embedded within this is a fancy word: actuarial. Apparently, it is a science: actuarial science. Practitioners are wizards in maths and stats and use them to assess risk. They calculate the odds of a natural disaster happening. But I was part of a lab experiment: these "scientists" had not got their calculations correct when it came to Christchurch. When tens of thousands of houses were wrecked, it caught them by surprise. They hadn't factored in enough risk. Insurance companies had issued policies to homeowners that allowed for replacement of the wrecked houses.

If the actuaries had got their algorithms right, they would have gone for "sum insured". This would have capped the amount the company would pay out, even if it was not enough to pay for building a replacement house. But they didn't. This meant the insurers had to reduce cost blowouts by compensating homeowners to the bare minimum. They prevaricated and misled claimants, hoping some would give up and accept low offers, simply go away, go mad, or die.

My own true loss is unquantifiable. My grief counsellor urges me to tote up my personal losses anyway. She thinks it will be helpful in seeing how utterly my life has changed. Here is what is gone: my daughter, Victoria McLeod; my health; my time; my money; my attention span; my happiness; my husband Malcolm's health and time; his happiness; holidays when we could have had fun together instead of schlepping to Christchurch to check on the progress, or lack of it, of the house build; my belief in the essential goodness and kindness of people.

The completed house is put up for auction but attracts no bids. I dismiss the property agent and engage a new one. Her slogan is "Trust in Trish". We have a mutual friend who lived in the same Singapore condo as us and knew Victoria when she was little. I hope this is a good omen.

Dealing with the house in Christchurch has involved lawyers, geotech engineering experts, formal documents, and becoming familiar with insurance jargon and building technicalities. Whether I had a living daughter to look after or a dead daughter to grieve for, hours had to be set aside each week for communication by email and perusal of replies, followed by googling to obtain information to seek solutions.

At least this was a process for which there would be an outcome: a house built. Coping with the loss of my daughter has had no such quantifiable process, despite psychologist Elizabeth Kübler Ross's famous five stages of grief: denial, anger, bargaining, depression and acceptance. It has not been neat and linear. Instead, multiple threads of feelings, reactions, reversions and existing have been intertwined like a giant ball of knitting wool.

In the years after the first traumatic anniversary of Victoria's death, no one from the school teaching faculty, board or student welfare team contacts us in any formal way to ask how we are doing or to honour our daughter. Victoria's piano teacher, who has long left the school, sends a photograph of Vic, aged around ten and smiling. This is the only message. Just as our insurance company has succeeded in reducing its damage limitation with our house, the school has succeeded in controlling any negative fallout from Victoria's death. The rolls are full. New buildings have popped up. I drive past and see students running around, wearing the uniform Victoria wore, full of life.

Grief and the concept of property as a shrine to a lost loved one rear their heads in Singapore, too. A scandal

SHRINES AND BOXES

to do with Singapore's first family, the descendants of Lee Kuan Yew, hits the headlines. I am recalled to work extra days on the newspaper, copyediting an endless flow of stories. The real estate of my headspace becomes occupied by the property of another family.

The controversy involves Lee's three children, the eldest of whom is now the prime minister, squabbling over their inheritance—in particular, the family home at 38 Oxley Road. The siblings take to Facebook to make public accusations and rebuttals, and even put up correspondence from senior ministers and public servants who would have assumed it would be kept private.

The house is an old bungalow now owned by the younger of the two brothers. Along with his sister, he is adamant that it was his father's wish to demolish the house and that this must be honoured. However, there is a strong argument that the site has wider significance beyond the family to the nation itself and should be preserved. The older brother, Prime Minister Lee Hsien Loong, is in this camp. The house was where many important decisions affecting Singapore's future were made. The ruling People's Action Party was founded in its basement. There are calls to have the house gazetted as a national monument.

The younger brother flourishes a late change in Lee's will as proof that Lee wanted the home demolished. The older brother questions the veracity of this seventh will. The younger brother then explodes the issue to include accusations of nepotism and abuse of ministerial power. Singaporeans, who would never dare make such accusations in public, are riveted.

Grief for a famous man becomes a domestic tragicomedy played out on social media. Meanwhile, the unmarried daughter continues to live with a few trusted servants in the vast house, rattling around amid the 1970s-era teak furniture of her famous father and mother. Outside the walls and gate, Singaporeans flock to take selfies.

Lee Kuan Yew loathed the thought of the house becoming some sort of shrine—he saw Singapore itself as his legacy. He is quoted as saying in *Hard Truths to Keep Singapore Going*: "I've told the Cabinet, when I'm dead demolish it. ... I've seen other houses, Nehru's, Shakespeare's. They become a shambles after a while ... You know the cost of preserving it? It's an old house ... damp comes up the wall." The comments about a decaying house hit home. My bedroom toilet has become blocked. A layer of foul sludge seeps across the floors as I tap on my laptop.

The controversy over Lee's bungalow makes me realise that Victoria's bedroom has become a shrine. Malcolm and I like being able to wander into it and feel a tug of connection, a sense of her presence lingering there. I take comfort in seeing her many bottles of nail polish on the dressing table, her favourite books on their shelves, and her framed photos—including a signed one of *The Sound of Music* actor Julie Andrews—on her desk. The room's undisturbed state gives us a feeling of continuity. Things are left just as they had been when Vic went out into the pre-dawn darkness and never came back.

It makes the departure a temporary thing. It suggests that Vic has "only slipped away to the next room", as the funeral speech staple "Death is Nothing at All" by Henry Scott-Holland describes it. In place of her physical presence, I nurture the hope that she will return. In a handwritten journal when she was fifteen, she said: "If I were dead now, I'd freeze time and zap myself back home, have a Pizza Hut cheese crust pizza, popcorn, cola and plenty of chocolate."

Dead people do not come by afterwards on a whim and eat pizza in their bedroom. I know that but am not ready to accept it. As a concession I pray for signs that Vic exists even ephemerally, as stardust in the night sky, or in the blue flourish of a kingfisher's wing. But mostly I hope that she will come back as her fully formed, tall and beautiful self. Her bed is made, ready for her to arrive and plonk herself down. Her phone is still charged, with Pizza Hut home delivery on the speed dial.

I go to New Zealand for three months. When I return, Vic's bedroom is like a mausoleum. There is now no sense of her presence. A layer of dust coats her belongings. The net curtains look dirty and shabby; the cats have torn them with their claws while chasing flying insects or sunbeams. The wooden floor is gritty under my bare feet. Cloth shoulder bags dangle on a door handle, their straps thinning and fraying. A purple raffia bag from Trade Aid has faded to pink.

Vic anticipated all this in a poem she wrote, entitled "Winter Mind". I hear her soft, Kiwi-tinged voice describing:

> Dust building on the spines of unopened books.
> The colour draining from floral patterned sheets
>   and curios
> In bedrooms like tea-dregs, giving way to crumpled
>   black clothes
> And silence.

Later, with Malcolm, I talk about this feeling of finality, of the room having given up the ghost. If Vic were to come back now, he says, she would laugh and say incredulously, "What are you still doing here?"

We sit on our worn sofas, bought when she was about eight, and look out over the other apartment blocks. No one stirs. No birds fly past. Maintenance workers have lopped off the lower limbs of all the trees, so now the birds, including the kingfishers, are higher, out of sight. Nor can I hear them. The whole apartment block has an absence of presence. Or, a presence only of absence.

37

MAKING MEANING

Time does *not* heal. One Friday when, unusually, I have a day off work, I return once more to the spot where Vic died. Beforehand, I deliberately read a diary entry of Vic's, written on a Friday a month and a half before her death, in which she visits the spot where she was to die:

> I left the house and walked to the other apartment block that had ten floors. I sat for an hour and I cried very quietly in a deadened sort of way. I knew my mum would be home soon, so I got up, and walked across the car park to the outside stairs. I felt the breeze, and everything came back. This kind of hopelessness that made me not care that I sat down in the shadow of a crevasse on those stone steps and looked up at the sky.

Victoria wrote this at night. When she looked up, she saw "more stars than I have ever seen in Singapore. It reminded me of New Zealand". I am there in the afternoon, and I see blue skies and a bright sun beginning its descent. The shadows start to grow longer, and already they are creating the exact "crevasse on those stone steps" that she refers to.

I feel immense sadness to think, on that Friday, I probably came home from work looking forward to the weekend, and would have been bright and chatty, and all the while Vic was suffering and could not tell me.

I refocus and try to analyse what was happening in Vic's mind when she wrote that, and when she had been at the actual spot. The words that leap out and torment me are "deadened" and "hopelessness". I can't think beyond those words. My bereaved self cannot delve further. Instead, I concentrate on what might have been a comfort to her. My daughter died here, but today, even in the shadows, it is a peaceful spot, overlooking tropical palm, tembusu and angsana trees on the hill opposite. I look to see if there was one tree that was special for my tree-lover. There is a tall old tree with a couple of bent branches and, on its trunk, a long gaping knot that looks like an open mouth. Vic had believed that trees could sometimes speak, so—despite all my evidence-based study on learning disorders—I resort to making meaning from the realm of the unexplained. I take this "mouth" shape as a sign to me that it lifted Vic's spirits in some way.

I take two photos with my phone. They are blurry but show the sun bursting through branches of the old tree—and the light from this forms the shape of a large heart. I had wanted to capture the tree and its surroundings, to peer later at the photos for any sign about why the place meant so much to Vic. But instead she sent me that glowing, branch-filled heart. Well, that's what a desperate mother wants to believe.

After I take the photos, I start to walk up the hill to our apartment block on the other side but turn to look back over to the tiled steps where Vic died. From the tree in front of me tumbles something blue, plunging to the ground. I gasp, then realise it is a kingfisher. It reaches the ground, snatches an insect in its beak, sits there vulnerable and exposed for a moment, and then flies up to a nearby branch. There it perches, quite calmly, the insect still alive and wriggling in its beak.

Three years after Vic's death, my diaries record more than a hundred sightings of kingfishers. It is surprising how often, if I am feeling down, I have seen one or sometimes two of these birds during my walks. Perhaps I have learnt to look for them. It helps that they are a distinctive colour. It can be a burst of blue across the greenery of the hill, or an aqua coat of feathers with a flash of white underbelly perched high up in a tree. Quite often, too, a kingfisher perches on the lowest limb of a tree nearest my apartment block. This is in the early morning, and the bird seems to be asleep. I can approach quite closely and stare up and take in its beauty. Once, I happen on two kingfishers on this branch. They are cooing gently to each other in an intimate language quite different from their usual shrieks of alarm.

The first Saturday I attend Bible study group at one

of the halls at St Ignatius church, a flash of Marian blue shoots past, into the branches of a nearby tree. I hear a shriek, answered by another. I am uplifted. I feel that some reassuring essence of Victoria is represented by their iridescent blue wings in flight.

Is there a message for me in these sightings? I hope so, as such things help me keep going, even if they don't seem rational. In the kingfisher's single-minded dive-bombing of prey is the sense that death is part of the natural order of things and can come quickly, unexpectedly, that life is fleeting and precious.

Or is there symbolism in the bird itself? Poet Charles Olson in "The Kingfishers" writes of the birds in a way that carries a message for humanity. He references the manner of their flight, in which they can be both in air and dive into water, and of their nests (which are in riverbanks or holes in trees, and which they line with regurgitated food): "And what is the message? The message is / a discrete or continuous sequence of measurable events distributed in time / is the birth of the air, is / the birth of water, is / a state between / the origin and / the end, between / birth and the beginning of / another fetid nest."

Olson wrote this poem in 1949, not long after the Second World War. The weekend before Victoria took her life, I remember asking her to name her favourite poem. She replied straight away with W.B. Yeats' 1918 anti-war poem "An Irish Airman Foresees His Death". At the time I thought it was an odd choice for a teenager of today's world, but I reasoned that Victoria must be studying it as part of English for HSC. However, I now realise that for Victoria it was an important poem, regardless of her studies. There are several aspects to this. First, war: she was deeply affected by Anne Frank's diaries of a teenager like herself, hunted down for her religion by fearsome and cruel soldiers. Second, civilisation's rise and fall: the prospect of trying to find a job in a corporate and calculating world. And third, her own inner battle, which was driving her to self-destruction.

All this made her despair about the future. She saw little point in fighting to overcome who she was. She knew we loved her, but it was not enough to battle her demons and keep living. She gave in. Immediate death seemed preferable to years of living. She established a pattern of repetitive, destructive thought that spiralled inwards and fed on itself. These lines from Yeats resonate: "A lonely impulse of delight / drove to this tumult in the clouds; / I balanced all, brought all to mind, / The years to come seemed waste of breath, / A waste of breath the years behind / In balance with this life, this death."

And as she wrote in her laptop journal fifteen days before she died, in her last ever entry: "I have let this cowardice envelop me, and I can't shake it off. I will commit the worst thing you can ever do to someone who loves you: killing yourself. The scary thing is, I'm okay with that."

She went on to rationalise that she was doing us, her parents, a favour—that she was a burden to us. Nothing could have been further from the truth. Without her, every waking hour of every day is overshadowed by her loss. It is something no amount of choice therapy, behavioural approaches and realigned mindsets can "fix". You can only accept it, seek kindness in yourself and others, take yourself out of yourself with acts of generosity, be positive, take pleasure in small things, find gratitude within the pain, and make some sort of a life around it.

I wonder if Victoria was really okay with her decision to kill herself. Perhaps she did not grasp the finality of death. At my meeting with Anna at the café she had run through a list of Vic's favourite singers, performers, songs and albums. The playlist that pumped from Vic's Android phone through her earbuds was the twenty-first-century teenager's equivalent of narrative discourse.

Look closer, Mum. It is Victoria's voice, as I lie in bed, remembering the meeting with Anna. I get out the diary where I wrote down Anna's list and consider it more deeply. I notice a new song: "My Immortal" by Evanescence, an American rock band. The song seems to be about a young woman who jumps to her death but whose self can't seem to leave the earthly world and haunts a friend or lover. The person left behind is aching in grief and desperate longing and the connection they still have with the departed one. They are so stricken they wish they could end it all.

I come across a video online that goes with the song. It's a black and white emo/goth-style clip. To haunting vocals, a young woman jumps, floats off a roof. A close-up shows her dead from the fall, every limb intact, her face unmarked and peaceful. The beautifully lit white cotton of her dress flutters in the breeze. Her dark hair is not sticky with blood. This glamourises death; you can come back and walk among the living and watch them suffer and this is cool.

I am aghast and want to warn people. Did Vic, despite her ruthless pragmatism about choosing the most efficient manner of suicide, harbour an illusion that she would be able to return to wander among us? At some deep neurological level, perhaps she—lover of haunting female vocals, devourer of cloying twentieth-century poems and stories—had not fully grasped the consequences of her actions. A 2012 study found that adolescents with ADHD had reduced volumes of anterior insular grey matter compared with a control group. Struggling with exams, self-esteem and social media isolation, Victoria may have been susceptible to images of ethereal young girls dying romanticised deaths.

Researcher Kathy Waldman explores this in an essay about anorexia. She writes about the illness's "perverse" literary tradition, "replete with ... glamorous elders (Emily Dickinson, Anne Sexton, Sylvia Plath), tropes (fairies, snow), and devices (paradox, irony, the unreliable narrator)".

Vic tried to starve herself, but this did not last. Then, her mind fastened directly on suicidal ideation. Both this and anorexia involve destruction of the self by the self. Waldman refers to anorexia as an "intellectual hallucination". Certainly, Vic's writing shows that she intellectualised her own death in a delusional way. Perhaps, despite all her research into anxiety and mental disorder, she did not really comprehend the finality and enormity of the fall. Or perhaps she did, but clung to the hope of immortality?

What am I to make of the voice, a month after Vic died, telling me to go to the ledge, where I found a heart scratched by her and the words "Bye Mum"? I may have imagined the voice, but the carved message was real enough. What of the message, two years later, to go to a different ledge, where I found a heart and a carved "M"? And what of the voice that guided me to find a page showing a serenely dead Snow White? Our relationship with the dead does not die with them. It keeps evolving. It is always there, re-framing the past, weighing down the present, and rendering the future one of conjecture about the now impossible.

I go for a tarot reading. It is oddly satisfying to have an older woman, a stranger, channelling figments of imagination to give me hope. Women have always done that for each other. She leads me to draw a scientifically illogical conclusion—one that, ironically, Vic would approve of. It is ungrounded in evidence-based science or even common sense. Vic's soul, she says, got fed up with the body, its neurological chaos, and simply left it behind. Something of Vic's consciousness remains present, either in me, or as itself.

38

MOVING AMONG US

"I'm free, I'm free." I had awoken to Victoria saying those words to me in a dream on that Monday when she died. But what if she hadn't been saying this to me in a dream, but was communicating to me in some way as she lay dying, or had already died?

If Victoria was dying or had just died, was my daughter, at some connected cellular-level, able to share thoughts? After all, studies have found that cells from a foetus cross over into the mother and remain throughout life. They become part of you. If identical twins can tell what the other is thinking or feeling even while apart, why not a mother and child, especially if particularly close? But if I had indeed received a message from Victoria that she felt free and happy, why had I not been aware beforehand that she was having suicidal thoughts and was committed to a carefully planned path of self-destruction? Where was the cellular-level connection then? And if not that, what about the much-vaunted maternal instinct?

If I think back, I see now that for at least a month—around the time of the parent-teacher meetings—I had felt a deep current of foreboding, as if the family was being drawn to a waterfall. However, I never stopped to examine it. I reached for simplistic explanations. I put Vic's detachment down to her being a moody teenager. I blamed my own lack of self-esteem and the "harried mother" syndrome for being off-putting to her. I assumed Malcolm's grumpiness was due to my nagging at him to go to bed earlier, and annoyance with how he prioritised work. I didn't know he feared he had cancer. And I probably assumed the force that tugged at my heart was worry about Victoria's final-year exams, and my sadness at the prospect of her leaving us to go and study in New Zealand—the prospect that this lovely person would no longer be around but out in the world, growing away from us.

A mother I came to know through attending bereavement support groups talked to me of feeling a similar worrying undercurrent in her life before her son died. It was such a deep tugging tide of darkness that one night she woke from a nightmare that she was stepping out into an abyss "as if in mid-air". It was so vivid that she stepped out of bed and broke her ankle as she fell to the floor. However, she did not connect this feeling of dread to her family, but to herself and worries about her future. Her son was in his first year of university in another country and she had thought he was doing okay. A few weeks after her dream he took his life, stepping into mid-air to hang himself.

Was the mother's dream a premonition? Or an awareness of a child's thoughts at some unconscious level?

Another possible reason for my sense that my daughter had communicated with me is that there may be a soul and that it exists beyond the containment of the physical self. If not a soul, then some formless but tangible consciousness. This could be for a short while, or it could be forever. One of my favourite poets, Marianne Boruch, writes in *The Little Death of Self*: "I begin with three ancient premises I almost believe. One; the dead move among us."

Note the use of the word "almost". I am sort of in that camp. I want to believe, there are signs in front of my very eyes, and yet it is not enough. Is this desire for irrefutable scientific evidence a good thing, or just a human-world failing?

Whatever the case, the message I received from Victoria the morning she died rocked me to my foundations. It raised the prospect that the extreme connection between mother and child might continue after death. Somehow, perhaps we were—are—able to communicate through extended consciousness. Certainly, just as I can't yet fully conceptualise Vic's death as her own self-annihilation, I can't believe her soul does not live on in some way. I can't believe that all that life, energy and potential has gone.

In the months after Vic died, I allowed myself to

follow this thread of thought and it reawakened the spiritual dimension in me.

However, the thought of new beginnings of any form scares me. For now, I can't even end things. I can't stand endings in any shape or form. But of course, there must always be endings.

One way to keep going—even if you are only avoiding an ending—is to not fall victim to the grief and let it define you. I put my grief to positive use by letting Victoria's journal writing make its way in the world so she might help others.

A long piece where Vic wrote—"I might not make this year. I know that when I see those grades bold and black on a piece of paper I will either jump for joy, or jump off the top floor of this condo"—appears in an Australian book about teenagers and exam pressure called *Beautiful Failures*. I struck up a friendship online with its author, *Guardian* editor Lucy Clark, when she wrote about the struggles of her own daughter within "our broken education system".

A short extract from Vic's journal that appeared in Singapore's *Sunday Times* drew over 50,000 hits in a few days. Comments included teens empathising with Vic's viewpoint about not being one of the "cool kids" and worries about pressure to study for exams.

A whole chapter is devoted to Victoria in the book *Suicidal: Why We Kill Ourselves* by American psychologist Jesse Bering, published by the University of Chicago Press. New Zealand-based Dr Bering analyses Vic's journal within the framework of new theories on teen suicide. As a result of this book, Victoria's writing has been praised in *New Yorker* magazine. In a review of the book in January 2019, writer Barrett Swanson said of Vic's journals, which are quoted in the book: "Victoria McLeod was herself a writer and, even at her young age, displayed a gimlet-eyed approach to the world and a winsome narrative persona. In her diary, Vic was at work on a profoundly important story, one that was asking all the right questions. ... It's impossible to know, of course, whether a better story would have saved her. The onus falls upon us to examine the ones we're telling."

This makes me reflect on what stories I am telling in this book. It occurs to me that Victoria has given me the gift of being able to tell her story, and also mine and Malcolm's. Grief can be a prison. In enabling me to write about her, Victoria has opened a door not only for my journey of grief to go out into the world to help others, but for the changed me to find a new identity. I'm letting the current take me to a place within myself that is more awakened to the world, in all its mysteries and possibilities.

39

NEW MOONS

But life has a habit of subverting everything. A Singapore colleague's nineteen-year-old niece takes her own life. I have met her once and seen an artistic, kind soul. She has a loving family, a spiritual framework, doctors and psychologists, but nearly a year after I meet her she is dead.

Like Victoria, she finds a quiet corner of a building complex. Like Victoria, there was a full moon. Later, the colleague tells me she once mentioned Victoria to her niece, who made one comment: "Was she lonely?"

Vic writes of looking back to when she first started wanting to die at fourteen:

> I was lonely. And I hated the feeling that everybody was watching me, waiting for me to lose. I was sick and tired of being this person with nothing to offer. Who was so terrified to even make a speech, I would have rather suffocated than go through with it. It was basically very low self-esteem. There's a point when

every part of you believes that you are hopeless, and you feel that your very existence isn't necessary.

Bones, memories, messages remain—and essentially a belief that she lives on in some way, a belief that is sustaining. Also sustaining is the kindness of some people who knew Victoria and are happy to say her name, to keep it alive in conversations, or honour her by making the most of their lives.

This is particularly the case with school friends such as Hannah, who is studying speech therapy, and Anna who is pursuing a career in operatic singing. We keep in contact via Facebook. Following their progress in life is not bittersweet as I am proud of them and the way they remember Victoria with dignity. Sophie, studying hotel management, messages this moving tribute: "At first when I heard the news of her death, I felt a huge amount of guilt and sadness. But over time I remembered her legacy of the best moments we had together and all the fond memories I had with her. Victoria would not want me to be sad, but to remember her for the amazing person she was."

They are getting on with making the most of who they are and what Vic's death taught them. They look to new moons, not full moons.

40

MISSING THE KINGFISHERS

I walk to the hill and see that, all around, leafy trees have become mere trunks, hacked and sawn. It may have been a safety measure. Severe storms have caused trees to topple across the island. People have been hurt, cars dented. The result, in my neck of the woods, is an absence. There's no rustling of leaves in a breeze. And the tree whose branches formed a heart backlit by the sun has gone. Its green majesty may have been the last thing Victoria saw as she died. Now it is just a stump. There are no birds in sight. No kingfisher sits poised on a nearby branch, looking for insects to swoop on. I can only hear their calls from high up, beyond sight, in the tallest trees that still have their canopies.

After a year on the market, the house in Christchurch finally sells to a migrant family from Britain with a five-year-old daughter who will most likely have the room once meant for Victoria. They love the house.

My last actuarial loss adjustment is to cancel a small life insurance policy for accidental death, benefiting

Victoria should I suddenly keel over. For four years after her death, I have kept paying the premium of a hundred dollars a month. One day, I see the pointlessness of this. The insurers ask why I am cancelling. I explain there is no longer a beneficiary.

Years pass, but I never hear from my brother, his wife and their two boys, although I think of them often. I am sure my brother thinks of me, and once in a dream I see him in a café and give him a hug. My parents email now and again, and out of the blue, when I turn sixty, five years after Victoria's death, my mother sends me a "Happy Birthday" card she has hand painted.

At the newspaper office there is a new CEO, a former army general turned corporate problem-solver. He has no hands-on newspaper experience, but amid digital disruption this is probably an advantage. Still, this outlier aspect is unnerving for the hardened hacks among his journalists. Singapore Press Holdings announces it will cut 250 jobs. I retain my job but lose friends and colleagues. The changes happen suddenly. People I've worked with for years are gone in a day.

I email Mary's mother on the chance that this time she will respond. I share a newspaper piece that quotes from Victoria's journals. She replies and thanks me for the piece. Her message includes the sad comment: "Mary has been suffering deeply for the last few years, although I do not want to expand upon that. Victoria's death is a component."

Vic wrote to Mary two days before she died:

Hey there Sunshine, this box is your Fix You First Aid Kit (with no sharp objects). And because I couldn't resist, here are a couple of Coldplay lyrics we used to sing, which I think are rather fitting...

Malcolm and I decide that Victoria's remains should be in New Zealand, where she was happy in nature, with family, away from the pressures of school. Malcolm carries the urn in a backpack from Singapore. He has rung a few airlines to ask about procedure (without going into the fact they are not ash but bones). Policies vary depending on the airline. Mostly, they ask that you be discreet and wrap things tightly. Carrying a Certificate of Cremation is advised, in case you are stopped by officials.

He learns it is quite common for relatives to transport ashes across continents and oceans so they can be scattered at a meaningful spot. At any time of day or night, up there in the sky, the remains of loved ones are hurtling at jet speed in overhead lockers as carry-on luggage, or in the hold in checked-in bags.

Scattering of ashes is not on our agenda. Bones don't scatter easily. Malcolm buries a handful under a tree at Kakanui. We keep the intact finger bones within the bowl of a Buddhist stupa in Victoria's bedroom there. Neither of us are Buddhists and yet we feel this is right. For the rest, we hold a small farewell service. A priest says thoughtful prayers. The gathering sings "The Lord Is My Shepherd". Each person places a sprig of lavender from Sheila's garden on the newly dug ground in which the urn is placed. We have erected a granite headstone engraved with a special poem of Victoria's. Fluttering pansies and nodding daffodils are a burst of performance art in a tub.

We take lavender back to Singapore and scatter the petals near where Victoria died. There is something circular to this that is fitting. Just how fitting I find out after the fifth anniversary of Victoria's death. A Filipina housekeeper, Marita Millada, lays flowers of remembrance at the site of Vic's death every anniversary. Marita often babysat Victoria when she was little. She is from the same province as Mae—Mindanao—and the two women are still in touch. Mae has a Mass said for Victoria every April 14.

When I get back from this annual trip to New Zealand, Marita visits to show me photos of the bouquets she bought and laid on the footpath where Vic died. Masses of orange gerbera, yellow puffball marigolds, purple and white orchids and little écru roses spill on to the tiles. The yellow and orange are outrageously cheerful in a way that loosens throats constricted by grief. We cry together.

Later, talking to Marita, I learn that she and little Victoria used to go to the very spot where she was to die, sit there and bundle up flowers they had picked from the adjacent planter box. Vic would have been five or six. Marita says she was "always laughing and chatting". They would place blooms of all colours on the ledge of the planter box and pretend to buy and sell them to each other.

Perhaps this is another clue as to why Victoria chose this spot to die. It was a place of safety, where she had been happy. Could it also be it was a place where she entered childhood, and chose not to leave it, or at least chose to leave it on her terms? Amid memories of laughter, yellow dahlias and bright orange gerbera blooms, her little self is there, encircled by tembusu and coconut palm trees, the kingfishers shrieking.

EPILOGUE

The Ōamaru cemetery is ringed by big old pine trees and paddocks of sheep. Six months before the fifth anniversary of Victoria's death, Grandma Sheila dies after a short illness and her ashes are placed there. She is with her husband, Jack McLeod—Victoria's grandfather. They rest on a slight rise that is a short walk away from Victoria.

After visiting Victoria, we call a cheery "Hello" from the car as we drive past. I don't know why we chorus out this slightly inane greeting. I suppose it is to lift ourselves from the sadness. Sometimes I see Malcolm kiss Victoria's headstone and mutter, "Stupid girl." My routine is to whisper, "Love you, darling."

We step back. There is room for this as we have purchased the plots on either side of Victoria. This is our final property purchase, a few square metres of soil in which will be buried urns or small boxes of ashes. It may seem grim to go about my life knowing the precise location of my future among the dead, but it is something I can accept.

EPILOGUE

My headstone will have a line both Vic and I liked from *The Lord Of The Rings*, in which Gandalf says, "white shores, and beyond, a far green country under a swift sunrise". This is how we see New Zealand, our thoughts drifting to home, to a people-free landscape of greenery and mountains, as we sit in Singapore, staring at the window grilles of the apartment block opposite. Perhaps our Taoist neighbour had similar yearnings, with his topography of the heart being in nature: the Guilin limestone mountains.

I am reminded of the Taoist duality of order and chaos as I look at the rows of the dead neatly laid out. Victoria's death, though, left behind only emotional chaos. I am bereft without her. But the essence of her that remains ensures the chaos is not meaningless.

Beyond the Ōamaru cemetery, fields and croplands give way to rolling hills leading to the Kakanui mountains, the backdrop also to the view from our cottage and where I once saw a shooting star. In summer, the mountains are hills of green. In winter, they are topped with snow and become gatekeepers to the interior.

Vic wrote a poem about how those left behind will look at the stars and asked that it be put on her headstone. "If I'm getting my 'affairs' in order, I might as well sort some things out. Before I become another statistic. My clothes and shoes (or whatever wearable ones) go directly to people who could never afford them. My books too. My mediocre poem 'I Will Be' be put on my headstone."

I Will Be
You look up. Stars—little lights
Little places where you
Cannot live with your
Lungs and your skin—
But with your heart.
My little world will meet
Yours, and yours mine.

I will be there as
Another dot to join the dots,
So that when you look up,
I will be there, and you know
I will be free.

Victoria McLeod

(December 27, 1996–April 14, 2014)

ACKNOWLEDGEMENTS

Thank you, foremost, to Awa Press and publisher Mary Varnham for your invaluable support; my tutor Chris Price at the International Institute of Modern Letters and my fellow students in the 2017 MA in Creative Writing course (poetry and creative non-fiction): Sarah Scott, Rebecca Priestley, Tayi Tibble, Sam Duckor-Jones, essa may ranapiri, Claire O'Loughlin, Sudha Rao, Jac Jenkins and Rebecca Reader; and also Emily Perkins and her fiction class, especially Maria Samuela, Lynne Robertson, Nicole Colmar and Clare Moleta. Thanks to my MA assessor Martin Edmond for his invaluable advice; to writer and artist Cushla Parekowhai; to St Dominic's College, Henderson, classmates Fiona and Estelle, who have always been there for me; to Kakanui friends Rhonda Chase, Claire Robertson, Bill Blair and Lyndsay Murray; and horse-rider Shirley Sheat and her late husband Bruce. Horses Tess and Hannah, and cats Mittens and Angelina. Thanks to all the people who consented to be interviewed or who helped with the research for his book, especially Victoria's friends who shared so generously—Hannah, Sophie, and their mothers; to performance artist Katherine McLeod, and Canadian writer and educator Jacyntha England.

ACKNOWLEDGEMENTS

A special thanks to Ethos Books, Singapore, and publisher Ng Kah Gay, the first publisher to take up *Loss Adjustment*; to writer and academic Dr Jesse Bering, Head of Science Communication at the University of Otago; and WellSouth Suicide Prevention Officer Bonnie Scarth. And most of all, my thanks to Malcolm, my fellow traveller.

WHERE TO GO FOR HELP

If you or someone you know is struggling or in crisis, here are hotlines and agencies recommended by the New Zealand Ministry of Health. All services are free, and are available 24 hours a day, 7 days a week unless otherwise stated.

For counselling and support
Need to talk? Free call or text 1737 any time
Lifeline – 0800 543 354
Samaritans – 0800 726 666
Healthline – 0800 611 116
Chinese Lifeline – 0800 888 880 (for people who speak Mandarin or Cantonese)

For children and young people
Youthline – 0800 376 633, free text 234 or email talk@youthline.co.nz (for young people, and their parents, whānau and friends)
What's Up – 0800 942 8787 (for 5- to 18-year-olds; 1 p.m. to 11 p.m.)

The Lowdown – visit thelowdown.co.nz, email team@thelowdown.co.nz or free text 5626 (emails and text messages will be responded to between 12 noon and 12 midnight)

SPARX – sparx.org.nz – an online self-help tool that teaches young people the key skills needed to help combat depression and anxiety

For help with specific issues

Depression.org.nz – includes sections for Māori and Pasifika, and The Journal, a free online self-help tool

OUTLine NZ – 0800 688 5463 (0800 OUTLINE) (for sexuality or gender identity issues; 9 a.m. to 9 p.m. weekdays, and 6 p.m. to 8 p.m. weekends)

Alcohol Drug Helpline – 0800 787 797 (for people dealing with an alcohol or other drug problem; 10 a.m. to 10 p.m.)

Women's Refuge Crisisline – 0800 733 843 (0800 REFUGE) (for women living with violence or fear in their relationship or family)

Shakti Crisis Line – 0800 742 584 (for migrant or refugee women living with violence or fear in their relationship or family)

Rape Crisis – 0800 883 300 (for support after rape or sexual assault)

PlunketLine – 0800 933 922 (provides support for new parents, including mothers experiencing postnatal depression)

For families, whānau, friends and supporters
Skylight – 0800 299 100 (for support through trauma, loss and grief; 9 a.m. to 5 p.m. weekdays)

Supporting Families In Mental Illness – 0800 732 825 (for families and whānau supporting a loved one who has a mental illness)

Mental Health Foundation – mentalhealth.org.nz – for information about supporting someone in distress, or looking after your own mental health and working towards recovery.